running a three-legged race across time

running a three-legged race across time

REALLIFESTUFFFORCOUPLES ON STAYING MARRIED

A NavStudy Featuring *The* MESSAGE®

Written and compiled by Tim McLaughlin

Our Guarantee to You

We believe so strongly in the message of our books that we are making this quality guarantee to you. If for any reason you are disappointed with the content of this book, return the title page to us with your name and address and we will refund to you the list price of the book. To help us serve you better, please briefly describe why you were disappointed. Mail your refund request to: NavPress, P.O. Box 35002, Colorado Springs, CO 80935.

The Navigators is an international Christian organization. Our mission is to reach, disciple, and equip people to know Christ and to make Him known through successive generations. We envision multitudes of diverse people in the United States and every other nation who have a passionate love for Christ, live a lifestyle of sharing Christ's love, and multiply spiritual laborers among those without Christ.

NavPress is the publishing ministry of The Navigators. NavPress publications help believers learn biblical truth and apply what they learn to their lives and ministries. Our mission is to stimulate spiritual formation among our readers.

ISBN 1-60006-018-8

Cover design by sutdiogearbox.com
Cover photo by Getty
Creative Team: Terry Behimer, John Blasé, Darla Hightower, Linda Vixie, Arvid Wallen, Laura Spray

Written and compiled by Tim McLaughlin.

Some of the anecdotal illustrations in this book are true to life and are included with the permission of the persons involved. All other illustrations are composites of real situations, and any resemblance to people living or dead is coincidental.

Printed in the United States of America

1 2 3 4 5 6 / 10 09 08 07 06

contents

about the **REAL**LIFE**STUFF**FOR**COUPLES** series

Let your love dictate how you deal with me;
　　teach me from your textbook on life.
I'm your servant—help me understand what that means,
　　the inner meaning of your instructions. . . .
Break open your words, let the light shine out,
　　let ordinary people see the meaning.

—Psalm 119:124-125,130

We're all yearning for understanding, for truth, wisdom, hope. Whether we quietly simmer in uncertainty or boil over into blatant unbelief, we long for a better life, a more meaningful existence, a more fulfilling marriage. We want our marriages to matter—to ourselves most of all, and then to our children and the rest of our families and friends. But real-life stuff—the urgency of daily life with all its responsibilities, major and minor catastrophes, conversations, dreams, and all—tends to fog up the image of the marriage we crave. And so we go on with the way things are.

We can pretend that there's really no problem, that everything is actually fine, thank you. We can intensify the same old way we've been living, hoping that more is better. We can flee—emotionally, spiritually, literally.

Whether or not we face it head-on, real life matters. In that fog there are things about ourselves, our spouses, and our marriages that cause distress, discomfort, and dis-ease.

The Real Life Stuff for Couples series is a safe place for exploring the truth about that fog. It's not your typical Bible study—no fill-in-the-blank questions, no one telling you what things mean or what to do. In fact, you'll probably finish a Real Life Stuff study with more questions than you started with. But through personal reflection and lively conversation in your small group (you know this is the best part of a Bible study, anyway), these books will take you where you need to go—and in the process bring greater hope and meaning to your life.

Each Real Life Stuff for Couples book gives you the space to ask the hard questions about marriage—yours and others'. A space to find comfort in the chaos. A space to enlarge your understanding of your marriage, your God, and where those two intersect.

And—with the guidance of the Holy Spirit—a space to discover real-life hope for your marriage that brings meaning to the everyday challenge of crafting a life together.

introduction

Marriage has many pains, but celibacy has no pleasures.

—Benjamin Franklin

There is pain in being single, in being married, and in being alive.
Marriage does, however, provide a person to blame for pain.

—Psychotherapist Roberta Temes in *Psychology Today* (May 1981)

Since God has so generously let us in on what he is doing, we're not about to throw up our hands and walk off the job just because we run into occasional hard times. We refuse to wear masks and play games. We don't maneuver and manipulate behind the scenes.

—2 Corinthians 4:1-2

"There are no happy marriages," said Garrison Keillor. "There are only marriages that keep trying, and marriages that stop trying." This is not as cynical as it may sound, depending on what you picture as *trying* in a marriage. To some trying is white-knuckling your way through a dreary marriage, hoping for a better future. To others trying is making the best of a marriage you had higher expectations for. To still others trying is tweaking your marriage regularly, in partnership with your spouse or individually.

However you picture trying—trying to establish a marriage, trying to redirect a marriage, trying to heal a marriage, trying to grow a marriage—it always requires communication. Sounds glib, but you know the truth of it. If you're striving for a marriage of mutual respect, mutual enjoyment, mutual love, mutual satisfaction—all these ideas that modern marriages have been laden with—you'll have to talk.

Talk about what? Marriage basics, such as what you and your spouse expect from your marriage. How closely your marriage approaches the model you've chosen. The degree of individuality you cede or retain in your marriage. Sex (always sex). The unrelenting influence on your marriage of your families of origin. And because those basics must be regularly renegotiated, talk about them from "I do" until "death parts us."

These issues will always be with us, at least as long as we as a culture or church—or you as a couple—want it all: a legal union, lifelong marital satisfaction, *and* romance. Or want even a modest slice of it all.

Think of this discussion guide as an encouragement to your starting out from whatever milepost you're just now reaching. You may be beginning your fifth year together, or fifteenth, or thirty-fifth. You may be starting out together on a new season in an otherwise established marriage—an empty nest, a big move, a birth, a death. Whatever the milepost marks, whether yours is a novice or a seasoned marriage, staying married will always require something of you.

Till death do you part, at least. Until then, refuse to wear masks with your mate; don't maneuver and manipulate your marriage. Do what you need to do to stay married—and every now and then, if you can, try to have some fun at it.

Not all of the excerpts and questions may directly apply to you and your marriage. Maybe you've always been married to the same person and a question about remarriage seems strange. Maybe a career is something you've never seriously pursued nor have a desire to. Maybe your marriage is in the early stages and crises really haven't reared their ugly heads yet. That's okay. The encouragement here is to go ahead and take the time to think through the questions. Maybe thinking through them will help you relate to the neighbors who are having serious crises. Maybe wrestling with some of these questions will give you insight into a son or daughter and their marriage questions. And maybe, just maybe, stepping into a question you didn't think applied to you may bring long buried feelings, desires, or issues to the surface. Just remember, this is a safe place to ask the hard questions about marriage; your marriage and others' as well.

how to use this discussion guide

This discussion guide is meant to be completed by you and your spouse—*and* in a small group of married couples. So before you dive into this book, put together a discussion group. Maybe the two of you already belong to a couples group. That works just fine. Or maybe you know three or four couples who could do coffee once a week. That works, too. Ask around. You'll be surprised how many of your coworkers, teammates, or neighbors would be interested in a small-group study, especially a study like this that doesn't require vast biblical knowledge. A group of three or four couples is optimal—any bigger and one or more members will likely be shut out of discussions. Or your small group can be only you two and another couple. Choose a couple who's not afraid to talk with you honestly and authentically about themselves. Make sure all participants have their own copy of this book.

1. *Read* the Bible passages and other readings in each lesson as a couple or on your own. Let it all soak in. Then use the white space provided to "think out loud on paper." Note content in the readings that troubles you, inspires you, confuses you, or challenges you. Be honest. Be bold. Don't shy away from the hard things. If you don't understand the passage, say so to your spouse, to your group. If you don't agree, say that, too. You may choose to cover a lesson in one

thirty- to forty-five-minute focused session. Or perhaps you'll spend twenty minutes a day on the readings.

2. *Think* about what you read. Think about what you wrote. Always ask, "What does this mean?" and "Why does this matter?" about the readings. Compare different Bible translations. Respond to the questions we've provided. You may have a lot to say on one topic, little on another. Allow the experience of others to broaden your experience. You'll be stretched here—called upon to evaluate what you've discovered and asked to make practical sense of it. In a group, that stretching can often be painful and sometimes embarrassing. But your willingness to be transparent—your openness to the possibility of personal growth—will reap great rewards.

3. *Pray* as you go through the entire session: before you read a word, in the middle of your thinking process, when you get stuck on a concept or passage, and as you approach the time when you'll explore these passages and thoughts together in a small group. Pray with your spouse, pray by yourself. Pray for inspiration, pray in frustration. Speak your prayers, write your prayers in this book, or let your silence be a prayer.

4. *Live.* (That's "live" as in rhymes with "give" as in "Give me something that will benefit my marriage.") Before you and your spouse meet with your small group, complete as much of this section as you can (particularly the "What I Want to Discuss" section). Then, in your small group, ask the hard questions about what the lesson means to you. (You know, the questions everyone is thinking, but no one is voicing.) Talk with your spouse about relevant, reachable goals. Record your real-world plan in this book. Commit to following through on these plans, and prepare to be held accountable.

5. *Follow up.* Don't let the life application drift away without action. Be accountable to the other couples in your group, and refer to previous "Live" sections often. Take time at the beginning of each new study to review. See how you're doing.

6. *Repeat* as necessary.

small-group study tips

After going through each week's study with your spouse, it's time to sit down with the other couples in your group and go deeper. Here are a few thoughts on how to make the most of your small-group discussion time.

Set ground rules. You don't need many. Here are two:

First, you'll want couples in your group to commit to the entire eight-week study. A binding legal document with notarized signatures and commitments written in blood probably isn't necessary. Just remember this: Significant personal growth happens when group members spend enough time together to really get to know each other. Hit-and-miss attendance rarely allows this to occur.

Second, agree together that everyone's story is important. Time is a valuable commodity, so if you have an hour to spend together, do your best to give each person ample time to express concerns, pass along insights, and generally feel like a participating member of the group. Small-group discussions are not monologues. However, a one-person-dominated discussion isn't always a bad thing. Not only is your role in a small group to explore and expand your own understanding, it's also to support one another. If someone truly needs more of the floor, give it to her. There will be times when the needs of the one outweigh the needs of the many. Use good judgment and allow a person extra time when needed. Your time may be next week.

Meet regularly. Choose a time and place, and stick to it. No one likes to arrange for a sitter, only to arrive at the study and learn that the meeting was canceled because someone's out of town. Consistency removes stress that could otherwise frustrate discussion and personal growth. It's only eight weeks. You can do this.

Talk openly. If you enter this study with shields up, you're probably not alone. And you're not a "bad person" for hesitating to unpack your life in front of friends or strangers. Maybe you're skeptical about the value of revealing the deepest parts of who you are to others. Maybe you're just not ready to say that much about that aspect of your marriage. Really, you don't have to go to a place where you're uncomfortable. If you want to sit and listen, offer a few thoughts, or merely hint at dilemmas in your marriage, go ahead. But don't neglect what brings you to this group of couples—that longing for a better, more satisfying, less tension-filled marriage. Dip your feet in the water of brutally honest conversation and you may choose to dive in. There is healing here.

Stay on task. Refrain from sharing information that falls into the "too much information" category. Don't spill unnecessary stuff, such as your wife's penchant for midnight belly dancing or your husband's obsession with Sandra Bullock.

If structure isn't your group's strength, try a few minutes of general comments about the study, and then take each "Live" question one at a time and give everyone in the group a chance to respond. That should quickly get you into the meat of matters.

Hold each other accountable. That "Live" section isn't just busywork. If you're ready for positive change in your marriage, take this section seriously. Not only should you be thorough as you summarize your discoveries, practical as you compose your goals, and realistic as you determine the plan for accountability, you must also hold the other couples in the group accountable for doing these things. Be lovingly, brutally honest as you examine each other's "Live" section. Don't hold back—this is where the rubber meets the road. A lack of openness here may send other couples in your group skidding off that road.

expectations

"I feel like if I keep my expectations for marriage high, I'll be disappointed . . . but having no expectations is just too dreary for me."

the beginning place

What we really want from our spouses (in no particular order):

Top 10 Things Wives Want from Their Husbands

- Telling her daily that she is loved
- Understanding and forgiveness
- Conversation
- Willingness to make time for her and your children
- Saying "yes" more than saying "no"
- Listening well
- Affection and kindness
- Sharing household and child rearing responsibilities
- A day off now and then
- Commitment to take care of yourself both physically and emotionally

Top 10 Things Husbands Want from Their Wives

- Believe in his capabilities
- Understanding
- Affirmation of his accomplishments
- Acceptance
- Less chatter
- Affection
- Respect
- Free time
- Trust
- To be a companion

From "Your Guide to Marriage," by Bob and Sheri Stritof[1]

There's not much here we don't know, right? Most obvious is the fuel for grimly humorous stereotypes: husbands want less chatter, wives want conversation; husbands want free time, wives want "a day off now and then." They're typical lists of marital expectations.

At one time in your marriage, if not now, "happily married" was a supreme hope. And you longed for not only a happy marriage, but also a lifetime marriage. Yet people change, marriages change, and spouses' expectations of their marriage and of each other change. The expectation of a twenty-three-year-old for lifelong, passionate love between intimate partners who share everything becomes at forty—well, something less. Sometimes a lot less. And after a decade or three of marriage, expectations can dissolve to simply making do.

This is not necessarily a bad thing or a sad thing. The trick is carving expectations to what is reasonable—whittle off too much, and marriage becomes dreary. Shave off too little, and you burn up your years in frustration.

And while we expect things of our spouses, what about marital expectations of ourselves? Rummage around in *that* drawer long enough, and you'll often find shame and deficiencies of self-esteem that are as debilitating as they are illusory.

So what do you expect of your marriage? What expectations do you lack? Have you lost any along the way? Would you like to create some? Which expectations conflict with those of your spouse? How explicitly or subtly do you and your spouse communicate your expectations? Use the space below to summarize your beginning place for this lesson. Describe how aware you are of the role expectations play in your marriage, list the expectations you find most frustrating, describe any longtime expectations you're just now recognizing, and explain how you and your spouse deal (or don't deal) with each other's expectations. We'll start here and then go deeper.

read what are your expectations attached to?

From the *Utne* article "Advice Columnist Carolyn Hax on Intimacy Today," by Anjula Razadan[2]

Razdan: What is the fate of traditional marriage, and what effect does that have on intimacy?

Hax: If people are detaching their expectations from a traditional bond, that's a good thing. So many people go into marriage expecting intimacy when, in fact, it's only a legal state. If you haven't established the intimacy, no marriage is going to get it for you. Of course, I just heard a traditionalist faint.

On the other side of it, if you're just saying, "Marriage isn't the answer, cuddle parties are," then you're going to be just as miserable as if you were married. If you haven't made the fundamental change inside you, you're never going to find it. You can be married and horribly lonely or you can be unmarried with your best friends and happily intimate. As long as there's been a need for closeness, people have been finding closeness—wherever it's presented itself.

think

- What is a traditional marriage to you?
- From what images or ideals did you compose your definition of a traditional marriage?
- Does intimacy make a marriage or does marriage create intimacy? Or is there a third sequence here?
- Hax believes that unless you learn how to create intimacy, neither a legal marriage nor lifelong flirting will make you happy. What do you think of this idea?
- Are you inclined to attach your expectations to, or detach them from, traditional marriage? If the latter, is this helping your marriage? Hurting it? Not making any difference?

think (continued)

pray

read being a provider: the modern version

From *Mars and Venus in Touch: Enhancing the Passion with Great Communication*, by John Gray[3]

Men really are seeking ways to make women happy and are just as interested as women in improved relationships. The problem is that their traditional ways of doing so aren't getting through to the women.

If problems arise at home, the traditional male approach to solving them is to become more successful at work. If a relationship is troubled, a traditional man doesn't take a seminar or purchase a book on relationships; he takes a course or buys a book on business or success. Why? Because from time immemorial, a man could always make his partner happier by being a better provider.

In hunter/gatherer days, this arrangement worked out fine. It worked well enough even for our fathers. For us, however, it doesn't work at all. Today's wives do not leave husbands because they're not being provided for. They leave because they are emotionally and romantically unfulfilled. When a man does not understand a woman's new needs, it is inevitable that she will be unfulfilled. This increased dissatisfaction is also what turns men off. Husbands do not leave wives because they no longer love them; they leave because they can't make them happy. Generally speaking, a man gives up on a relationship when he feels powerless to succeed in fulfilling his partner.

By understanding how circumstances have changed for both sexes, we can gain the insight and compassion necessary to master new approaches to mutually supportive relationships. . . .

Down through the centuries, women have looked to men for protection because it was crucial to their family's survival. This protector role carries over into our generation of relationships, but now, as we've said, it is more linked to emotional security. It means that she can talk without worrying about hurting him and without reprisal. It means that she can be in a bad mood without her mate's holding it against her or ignoring her.

think

- According to Gray, why do wives today leave their husbands? Why do husbands leave their wives?
- Compare your own observations of marriages with Gray's take on why couples split. Have you found his analysis accurate?
- No longer, says Gray, can a man make his wife "happier by being a better provider." Do you think this is a loss or that it's about time such a reason for marriage changed? Talk about this.
- Is emotional security what a wife today needs most from her husband, rather than physical security? Why or why not?
- In all of this, do you see—or in your heart, do you sense—a disconnect? Is our society trying to construct modern marriages on obsolete assumptions? Talk about this.

pray

read marital expectations: a short list

From *Good Advice*, by Todd Temple and Jim Hancock[4]

A couple of hints:

- There are no operational manuals for marriage. What you learn at home may or may not prepare you for your own marriage. Know going in that you'll produce an original because you and your mate are originals.
- Expect it to take years, maybe a decade or more, of concentrated work to produce the kind of marriage that will still be happy after 50 or 60 years. Know that it's time well spent.
- The single most important element in good marriages is friendship. Romance is up and down, physical attractiveness is subject to the law of gravity, success comes and goes, but friendship—ah, friendship. It grows and flowers to the end.

think

- In this reading, what resonates most with you? Least? Why?
- If you were offering teenagers (the target audience of this excerpt) three things they ought to expect in marriage, what would they be?
- In what sense are you and your spouse creating your own marriage from scratch "because you and your mate are originals"—and in what sense are you following a blueprint? Are both approaches valid? Both effective? Both biblical? Talk about this.
- Does the idea of friendship being the only constant in a marriage light your fire? Give you the chills? What?

think (continued)

pray

read suitable companion

Genesis 2:18-25

> GOD said, "It's not good for the Man to be alone; I'll make him a helper, a companion." So GOD formed from the dirt of the ground all the animals of the field and all the birds of the air. He brought them to the Man to see what he would name them. Whatever the Man called each living creature, that was its name. The Man named the cattle, named the birds of the air, named the wild animals; but he didn't find a suitable companion.
>
> GOD put the Man into a deep sleep. As he slept he removed one of his ribs and replaced it with flesh. GOD then used the rib that he had taken from the Man to make Woman and presented her to the Man.
>
> The Man said,
>
> "Finally! Bone of my bone,
> flesh of my flesh!
> Name her Woman
> for she was made from Man."
>
> Therefore a man leaves his father and mother and embraces his wife. They become one flesh.
>
> The two of them, the Man and his Wife, were naked, but they felt no shame.

think

- In this facet of the Creation story, what is the ancient writer trying to tell us?
- What was God's first attempt at giving the first man a companion? Choose a word to describe God's attempt.
- What expectations for your marriage does this part of the Creation story communicate? Does it say anything at all about marital expectations? Talk about this.
- What aspects of this first marriage do we have today? What aspects have disappeared? Is this a loss or a gain?

think (continued)

pray

read there's passion, then there's passion

Genesis 26:8-9

> One day, after they had been there quite a long time, Abimelech, king of the Philistines, looked out his window and saw Isaac fondling his wife Rebekah. Abimelech sent for Isaac and said, "So, she's your wife."

From *Abba's Child: The Cry of the Heart for Intimate Belonging*, by Brennan Manning[5]

> The etymological root of "passion" is the Latin verb *passere*, "to suffer." The passion of Jesus in his dialogue with Peter ["Do you love me?"] is "the voluntary laying oneself open to another and allowing oneself to be intimately *affected by* him; that is to say the suffering of passionate love."

think

- Do you think passion in a marriage between Christians is underrated or overrated? Why?
- Would you describe most of the Christian marriages you know as "passionate"? If not, why not?
- "Allowing oneself to be intimately affected by" another—what is your response to this definition of passion?
- Do you believe that husbands and wives should be intimately affected only by each other? Or do you think there is room for being affected intimately though nonsexually by someone other than your spouse?

think (continued)

pray

read disappointed expectations

From *Secret Longings of the Heart*, by Carol Kent[6]

She believed that marriage to a Christian man would mean living in a happy and fulfilling emotional, sexual, spiritual, and intellectual relationship with her best friend. Nancy expected the intellectual intimacy of her courtship to continue after the wedding. She realized her husband did not grow up in a family that expressed physical affection very often, but in her optimism she was sure that would change after the wedding. She expected to marry a tender lover who would combine a caring touch, affirming words, a clean body, and a deep physical desire for her alone.

think

- List one or two expectations you brought into marriage. How have they fared?
- Which marital expectation evaporated the quickest once you married?
- Do you think expectations ought to be reachable goals or unattainable ideals you work toward? Why?
- How would you advise Nancy if, after twenty years of such disappointed expectations, there was no change in her marriage?

think (continued)

pray

LIVE

what i want to discuss

What have you discovered this week that you definitely want to discuss with your small group? Write it here. Then begin your small-group discussion with these thoughts.

so what?

Use this space to summarize what you've discovered about expectations in your marriage. Review your "Beginning Place" if you need to remember where you started. How does God's truth impact the next step in your journey?

then what?

What is one practical thing you can do to apply what you've discovered? Describe how you will put this into practice. What steps will you take? Remember to think realistically; an admirable but unreachable goal is as good as no goal. Discuss your goal with your small group to further define it.

how?

Identify how you will be held accountable to the goal you described. Who will be on your support team? What are their responsibilities? How will you measure the success of your plan? Write the details here.

models

"I'm told the Bible is a marriage manual—but either I'm from a different planet, or I'm not being told the whole truth about what my marriage should look like. Or should it look like anything other than what we make it?"

the beginning place

If you want to succeed at anything in life—money management, child rearing, determining personal priorities, education, marriage—many Christian pastors and authors teach us to look to the Bible. If it is indeed the Word of God, then what it says about anything should be valued above everything else.

When it comes to marriage, the biblical model is clear: lifelong fidelity to one spouse of the opposite sex, right? (That, or lifelong celibacy.) And, many Christians believe, husbands should have a loving authority in the home; when push comes to shove in decision making, wives should show respectful submission to their husbands' headship.

The apostle Paul makes this clear in the many letters he writes to encourage new first-century Christians, to help them over the hump of their pagan or Jewish habits, to extinguish heresies.

But once you leave that thin section of your Bible (the New Testament's apostolic letters, from whence springs most modern Bible teaching on marriage, actually accounting for only 8 percent of your Bible), marriage models begin looking—well, interesting. A little messy, a little exotic, more different from than similar to our twenty-first-century Western understanding of marriage.

Take Adam and Eve—no civil ceremony, they just got together, thanks to Yahweh playing matchmaker. Abram? Married his half sister Sarai, then slept with other women, Hagar most notably, and numerous concubines who gave him children. Isaac's wife was selected for him—and not even by his father, but by his father's servant. (The lucky girl was a cousin of the groom, by the way.) Jacob was part of a patriarchal fivesome, what with his two wives and each of their maids.

Of Moses' marriage we know nothing other than the name of his wife (Zipporah), the fact that it was she, not Moses, who circumcised their son, and that she was apparently sent home to her father by Moses early in the Israelites' forty-year wilderness trek. King David collected wives like he collected military victories, and his most memorable son came from his affair with a married woman. The prophet Hosea married a whore who continued her extramarital activities.

So what do we have as a biblical model for marriage? Depends on where you are in the Bible: in ancient marriages in foreign cultures as described in the Old Testament, marriage models are all over the road. There is virtually nothing in the teachings of Jesus about marriage beyond answers to critics' questions about the legal intricacies of marriage, divorce, and remarriage.

That leaves us with the letters of the New Testament: relatively direct, specific, hard-and-fast exhortation about marital roles, duties, and attitudes. Understandably, most modern Bible teaching on marriage comes from this portion of Scripture, and the rest—the ancient, exotic, foreign, messy, Old Testament stuff—is usually spiritualized into metaphors that support the apostles' teaching.

Realize that your marriage model is not exclusively biblical, however you define it. You have witnessed marriages throughout your life—probably most influential, the marriage of your parents, then the marriages of other family members, and the marriages of friends. You have seen marriages start, stumble, thrive, endure, end. From all of these, you construct an image of what you want your marriage to be like.

So what models for marriage have been passed on to you? Taught to you? Ingrained in you? Offered to you? What have you always wanted your marriage to look like? Where did that image come from? Does it matter? Use the space below to summarize your beginning place for this lesson. Describe what you believe a marriage should look like, how closely or distantly your marriage conforms to this image, and how you feel about that. You may also want to describe the kinds of marriages you admire and whether or not your marriage resembles them. We'll start here and then go deeper.

read the american ideal

From the *Utne* article "Dancing with Monogamy," by Nina Utne[1]

> "I have come to see that our contemporary American ideal—courtship leading to the monogamous, isolated nuclear family—is just one option. And that in trying to hold onto this as the one and only way, we disregard all the evidence of dating disasters, unhappy marriages, and train-wreck divorces. We could be asking how we can find intimacy in new forms that are based on truth and integrity—and that truly promote happiness and well-being."

think

- How many models of marriage did you grow up thinking there were? What were they?
- How do you reconcile—or do you think that you even need to reconcile—two obvious facts that Utne reminds us of: the contemporary American monogamous ideal and the high failure rate of such marriages (whether measured by divorce or by unhappiness or unhealthiness within the marriage)?
- Do you think other options for intimacy can be compatible with a Christian marriage?
- List and describe some healthy marriages that are based on a model different from yours.

think (continued)

pray

read not for everyone

Matthew 19:3-12

One day the Pharisees were badgering him: "Is it legal for a man to divorce his wife for any reason?"

He answered, "Haven't you read in your Bible that the Creator originally made man and woman for each other, male and female? And because of this, a man leaves father and mother and is firmly bonded to his wife, becoming one flesh—no longer two bodies but one. Because God created this organic union of the two sexes, no one should desecrate his art by cutting them apart."

They shot back in rebuttal, "If that's so, why did Moses give instructions for divorce papers and divorce procedures?"

Jesus said, "Moses provided for divorce as a concession to your hardheartedness, but it is not part of God's original plan. I'm holding you to the original plan, and holding you liable for adultery if you divorce your faithful wife and then marry someone else. I make an exception in cases where the spouse has committed adultery."

Jesus' disciples objected, "If those are the terms of marriage, we're stuck. Why get married?"

But Jesus said, "Not everyone is mature enough to live a married life. It requires a certain aptitude and grace. Marriage isn't for everyone. Some, from birth seemingly, never give marriage a thought. Others never get asked—or accepted. And some decide not to get married for kingdom reasons. But if you're capable of growing into the largeness of marriage, do it."

think

- "Marriage isn't for everyone." How does that line up with the commonly heard idea that a spouse completes you—implying that singleness is somehow incomplete?
- What do you think is "God's original plan" that Jesus mentioned?

- What do you make of Jesus' speaking of a man leaving his father and mother for his wife—rather than a wife leaving her father and mother for her husband?
- Would you say this Bible passage is about marriage or divorce? Why?

pray

read heads

1 Corinthians 11:3-12

In a marriage relationship, there is authority from Christ to husband, and from husband to wife. The authority of Christ is the authority of God. Any man who speaks with God or about God in a way that shows a lack of respect for the authority of Christ, dishonors Christ. In the same way, a wife who speaks with God in a way that shows a lack of respect for the authority of her husband, dishonors her husband. Worse, she dishonors herself—an ugly sight, like a woman with her head shaved. This is basically the origin of these customs we have of women wearing head coverings in worship, while men take their hats off. By these symbolic acts, men and women, who far too often butt heads with each other, submit their "heads" to the Head: God.

Don't, by the way, read too much into the differences here between men and women. Neither man nor woman can go it alone or claim priority. Man was created first, as a beautiful shining reflection of God—that is true. But the head on a woman's body clearly outshines in beauty the head of her "head," her husband. The first woman came from man, true—but ever since then, every man comes from a woman! And since virtually everything comes from God anyway, let's quit going through these "who's first" routines.

think

- Do you think Paul comes down on the side of women, men, both, or neither? Why?
- Trace the different ways the apostle uses the word head in this passage.
- "Neither man nor woman can . . . claim priority," wrote Paul. Does this fit your idea of a Christian model of marriage? Why?
- Do we have a modern cultural equivalent of women wearing hats in worship (thereby covering their heads) and men

removing their hats? Are there any other ways we have of symbolically submitting our literal heads to the Head?

pray

read multiple models

From the *National Catholic Reporter* article "Many Models of Marriage Can and Do Exist," by Jeannette Cooperman[2]

> Marriage is splintering into a thousand different shapes. There are—as there have always been—marriages of convenience and marriages of common law; arranged marriages and platonic marriages and polygamous marriages. There are couples living together who gauge how married they feel by their mood (and whether their partner left dishes congealing in the sink). There are marriages in front of God and everybody, marriages that do the modern equivalent of waving blooded sheets because the couple believes the entire community has a stake in their union. There are marriages with prenuptial contracts so coldly detailed even the justice of the peace blanches. . . .
>
> Marriages are no different from friendships: They exist in varying degrees of intensity, some lives overlapping in virtually every detail, others intersecting once or twice or meeting at the edges. The human personality contains far too many variables to expect a single model in any relationship category. . . .
>
> The key, it seems to me, is recognizing what glue is powerful enough to bind your lives together and then honoring that bond, filling the cracks, scraping clean what crumbles, smoothing the sharp edges so no one gets hurt. Kept in good repair, any relationship can stay strong. Forget the details: God lives in the bond itself, and the resilience it makes possible. . . .
>
> I do believe marriage should last a lifetime; not only is love more fulfilling as it deepens, but it is nerve-wracking to imagine years of effort dissolved by someone clapping and announcing, "I divorce you" three times—or hiring a good lawyer and signing a piece of paper. Yet I have urged friends to split because the damage done is greater when they stay together and slowly gouge out each other's hearts.
>
> Maybe I'm a polygamist—I don't believe a marriage ever really ends, but I do believe people should separate, and I can't

rule out remarriage. So there: simultaneous multiple monogamies, one expressed, the other tacit and historical. Yet another version of marriage to add to the list.

think

- What glue is powerful enough to bind together the lives of you and your spouse? How do you and your spouse honor this "glue"?
- Have you ever felt torn, as Cooperman describes, believing that marriage should last a lifetime—yet reluctantly urging (or wanting to urge) a friend or family member to divorce because of the damage happening in the marriage? If so, what did you do? Or want to do?
- How significant is the difference between polygamy and one-at-a-time multiple marriages during one's lifetime?
- "God lives in the bond" of marriage, Cooperman claims. What do you think she means by this?

pray

read no thanks, ward

From *Why Marriage Matters: Reasons to Believe in Marriage in a Postmodern Society,* by Glenn T. Stanton[3]

[A] "real world" view of marriage needs to be recovered so people know what they are committing to. Otherwise, disappointment will be inevitable and people will continue to exit marriage when their false dream has gone bad. It should be the widespread understanding of our culture that marriage is the "toughest job you'll ever love" and that it is this very process that, paradoxically, makes it so rich. . . .

I am not arguing for a return to some nostalgic "June and Ward Cleaver" picture of family life. This lazy assumption is often made whenever there is a call for a return to strong marriages and families. Men and women simply do not relate to each other the way they did forty years ago, and I'm not necessarily suggesting a return to that era. Rather, I'm calling for a return to the idea that the marriage commitment be worked at and honored. I'm arguing for a return to the idea where children can count on their mom and dad being present in the same home, where family members and friends expect us to hang in there and make our marriage relationships work.

think

- How would you define a "real-world" view of marriage?
- Imagine that you're constructing a marriage model using aspects of June and Ward Cleaver. What would you keep? What would you throw away?
- Think for a moment how your male and female peers relate to each other. How is this different from how your grandparents' peers related to each other?
- How would you respond to someone who said, "If a business had a 50 percent failure rate, it would be shut down. Instead, society spends a lot of its time trying to keep marriage afloat and viable."

think (continued)

pray

read equals

1 Peter 3:1-6

> The same goes for you wives: Be good wives to your husbands, responsive to their needs. There are husbands who, indifferent as they are to any words about God, will be captivated by your life of holy beauty. What matters is not your outer appearance—the styling of your hair, the jewelry you wear, the cut of your clothes—but your inner disposition.
>
> Cultivate inner beauty, the gentle, gracious kind that God delights in. The holy women of old were beautiful before God that way, and were good, loyal wives to their husbands. Sarah, for instance, taking care of Abraham, would address him as "my dear husband." You'll be true daughters of Sarah if you do the same, unanxious and unintimidated.

think

- What is the apostle Peter's primary recommendation to wives?
- To husbands?
- How much distance is there between your culture's standards of marriage and Peter's? Why do you say that?

pray

LIVE

what i want to discuss

What have you discovered this week that you definitely want to discuss with your small group? Write that here. Then begin your small-group discussion with these thoughts.

so what?

Use the following space to summarize what you've discovered about the templates that couples use to model their marriage after. Review your Beginning Place if you need to remember where you began. How does God's truth impact the next step in your journey?

then what?

What is one practical thing you can do to apply what you've discovered? Describe how you will put this into practice. What steps will you take? Remember to think realistically; an admirable but unreachable goal is as good as no goal. Discuss your goal with your small group to further define it.

how?

Identify how you will be held accountable to the goal you described. Who will be on your support team? What are their responsibilities? How will you measure the success of your plan? Write the details here.

mine

"I'm beginning to resent that moment in my wedding when, after lighting our unity candle, we blew out our own candles."

the beginning place

"Joined in holy matrimony": Culture seems to have the upper hand in defining this phrase. Older cultures witnessed not only the bride and groom being joined, but their families and (here was the real point of it) their families' properties. Business alliances and property acquisitions were sealed in ancient times not by lawyers in a conference room, but by priests at an altar.

Legal identities were joined by marriage then, and now: It's still customary for a wife to take her husband's surname (though few social repercussions exist anymore should she choose not to assume his name). A couple may choose that the government views them as a single legal entity and file a joint return. Spouses may share a name, a tax return, a bed, a child. Ours is stamped on much in a marriage.

But is that possessive pronoun stamped on everything? Should it be stamped on everything? And if not, how does a couple distinguish among things ceded to the other, things retained by oneself, and things shared?

Take spirituality, for instance. When a woman marries, does she become less responsible for her inner life, for her spiritual well-being? When a man marries, does he somehow absorb responsibility for his wife's relationship with God?

"At the resurrection we're beyond marriage," Jesus taught. "As with the angels, all our ecstasies and intimacies then will be with God" (Matthew 22:30).

Let's follow that logic for a moment. At the resurrection of the dead we are, in Jesus' words, beyond marriage. Is it reasonable to conclude that we are essentially and fundamentally individuals, although perhaps now bound to another in a strictly temporal though God-ordained arrangement called marriage?

If that is the case, then marriage is like a career—not an eternal end-all-be-all, but one of several means of acquiring grace during our mortal existence, en route to ultimate union with God. Anything that you ceded to your spouse at your wedding was only for a season, only for the duration of this life.

Enough of the theorizing. All you'd like to know is, "Can I have a God-honoring marriage and still invest time or money or my intellect or my emotions in something just me and not us?" And here a gender distinction exists, at least in our culture: There is truth in the stereotype of the husband's poker or bowling night, his weekend golf game, or meeting his cronies at the pub. But what about wives? A monthly mom's day out, complete with free child care provided by your church, is a nice gesture, but most women would be quick to say, "It just doesn't cut it."

So how are you navigating the territory of mine-yours-ours in your marriage? Or to use another metaphor: Do you have any desire to now and then dance apart instead of together? Not necessarily with someone else, just apart. When you married, how closely do you think your identity was melded to that of your spouse? How comfortable are you with that? Use the space below to summarize your beginning place for this lesson. We'll start here and then go deeper.

read wherever you go

Ruth 1:8-18

After a short while on the road, Naomi told her two daughters-in-law, "Go back. Go home and live with your mothers. And may God treat you as graciously as you treated your deceased husbands and me. May God give each of you a new home and a new husband!" She kissed them and they cried openly.

They said, "No, we're going on with you to your people."

But Naomi was firm: "Go back, my dear daughters. Why would you come with me? Do you suppose I still have sons in my womb who can become your future husbands? Go back, dear daughters—on your way, please! I'm too old to get a husband. Why, even if I said, 'There's still hope!' and this very night got a man and had sons, can you imagine being satisfied to wait until they were grown? Would you wait that long to get married again? No, dear daughters; this is a bitter pill for me to swallow—more bitter for me than for you. God has dealt me a hard blow."

Again they cried openly. Orpah kissed her mother-in-law good-bye; but Ruth embraced her and held on.

Naomi said, "Look, your sister-in-law is going back home to live with her own people and gods; go with her."

But Ruth said, "Don't force me to leave you; don't make me go home. Where you go, I go; and where you live, I'll live. Your people are my people, your God is my god; where you die, I'll die, and that's where I'll be buried, so help me God—not even death itself is going to come between us!"

When Naomi saw that Ruth had her heart set on going with her, she gave in. And so the two of them traveled on together to Bethlehem.

think

- Did you recognize some classic wedding words nested in this Bible passage? What are they?
- Do you think that the context of the words strains their application these days? Why?
- What aspects of marriage are these words intended to reinforce and illustrate?
- Do Ruth's words accurately describe the spirit of today's marriages—does today's bride follow her new husband to his home, do his people become her people, his God her God? If they don't, should this sentiment describe a modern marriage?

pray

read a new creature

From *Two-Part Invention: The Story of a Marriage*, by Madeleine L'Engle[1]

> I do not think that death can take away the fact that Hugh and I are "we" and "us," a new creature born at the time of our marriage vows, which has grown along with us as our marriage has grown. Even during the times, inevitable in all marriages, when I have felt angry, or alienated, the instinctive "we" remains. And most growth has come during times of trial. Trial by fire.

think

- Some people think that there are not just two, but three entities in a marriage: wife, husband, and the marriage itself—and all three must be deliberately nurtured and tended. What is your gut response to this idea?
- Describe a time in your marriage when the "we" and the "us" blocked, stifled, or stunted the "me" and the "I."
- Do you look at that time as selfish or valid? Why?
- How did you deal with that time?
- Think of the marriages you admire. How do you think they deal with times like that?

pray

read close, but not too close

From the poem "On Marriage" in *The Prophet*, by Kahlil Gibran[2]

Then Almitra spoke again and said, "And what of Marriage, master?"
And he answered saying:
You were born together, and together you shall be forevermore.
You shall be together when white wings of death scatter your days.
Aye, you shall be together even in the silent memory of God.
But let there be spaces in your togetherness,
And let the winds of the heavens dance between you.
Love one another but make not a bond of love:
Let it rather be a moving sea between the shores of your souls.
Fill each other's cup but drink not from one cup.
Give one another of your bread but eat not from the same loaf.
Sing and dance together and be joyous, but let each one of you be alone,
Even as the strings of a lute are alone though they quiver with the same music.
Give your hearts, but not into each other's keeping.
For only the hand of Life can contain your hearts.
And stand together, yet not too near together:
For the pillars of the temple stand apart,
And the oak tree and the cypress grow not in each other's shadow.

think

- What image from this passage resonates most with you? Why?
- What here seems most true to your experience? What seems most distant from your experience?
- Is there anything here not your experience, but you'd like it to be? Why?

- How would you respond to someone who said, "A married couple should try to stand as closely together as possible. How else can they experience the safety, the partnership, the union—emotionally, spiritually, physically—of their marriage?"

pray

read living in the rhythms of creation

From *The Red Tent*, by Anita Diamant[3]

> [Said Jacob's wife Leah to her daughter Dinah,] "The flow at the dark of the moon, the healing blood of the moon's birth—to men, this is flux and distemper, bother and pain. They imagine we suffer and consider themselves lucky. We do not disabuse them.
>
> "In the red tent, the truth is known. In the red tent, where days pass like a gentle stream, as the gift of Innana courses through us, cleansing the body of last month's life, women give thanks—for repose and restoration, for the knowledge that life comes from between our legs, and that life costs blood.". . . [158]
>
> The four sisters [Leah, Rachel, Zilpah, and Bilhah—the wives of Jacob] spoke of these things in the red tent, which they always entered a day before the rest of the women in the camp. Perhaps their early years together when they were the only women in camp created a habit in their bodies that brought on the flow of blood some hours before the bondswomen. Or perhaps it was simply the need of their hearts to spend a day among themselves. . . . [62]
>
> With every new moon, I took my place in the red tent and learned from my mothers how to keep my feet from touching the bare earth and how to sit comfortably on a rag over straw. My days took shape in relation to the waxing and waning of the moon. Time wrapped itself around the gathering within my body, the swelling of my breasts, the aching anticipation of release, the three quiet days of separation and pause. . . . [175]

think

- In nomadic cultures—in this case, also an ancient one—the only schedules are those dictated by the natural world. Seasons for planting, for reaping, for letting lie fallow. Seasons for breeding, for pasturing, for slaughtering. Seasons for sex, seasons for abstinence. Do any parts of your life still correspond to the rhythms of the natural world? If so, is this by necessity or by choice?

- Should "down time" include temporary separateness from some relationships, too? If so, which relationships? Why?
- What would your inner response be on hearing these words from a respected modern matriarch: "There's no way our marriage would have survived for these forty years if we hadn't taken regular breaks from each other"?
- What would occasional, regular separateness look like in our twenty-first-century marriages? Give yourself the freedom to fully imagine this.

pray

read equals

1 Peter 3:7

> The same goes for you husbands: Be good husbands to your wives. Honor them, delight in them. As women they lack some of your advantages. But in the new life of God's grace, you're equals. Treat your wives, then, as equals so your prayers don't run aground.

think

- If a wife and her husband are indeed equals "in the new life of God's grace," what does this imply about what they each ceded, retained, or shared when they got married?
- What might Peter have meant by his remark that women lack some of the advantages of men? How do you, from your perspective, interpret those words now?
- How literal do you think the apostle was being when he wrote that if husbands do not treat their wives as equals, their prayers will "run aground"? Is there actually a marital qualification for answered prayers? Talk about this.

pray

read is it or isn't it my career?

From *Secret Longings of the Heart*, by Carol Kent[4]

> My engagement was announced last week, and in three months I'll be married to a seminary student. My degree is in business administration, and I'm planning a career in marketing and sales. I think I can be a pastor's wife *and* a businesswoman, but I keep running into people who are shocked with that thought. I know several pastors' wives who are teachers or nurses, but the thought of a pastor's wife in business seems to scare people. Why shouldn't I be allowed to pursue what I'm best at without struggling under the expectations of individuals who define the role of the pastor's wife differently than I do?

think

- What do you think is the wisest track for this woman to follow—pursue a business career and deal with the flak? Or put her career on hold while her husband settles into his career, then resume hers later?
- What would you do if you were this woman? Why?
- Compare this woman's desire to enter business with her husband's desire to enter the ministry. How do you weigh those careers against each other? How do you think most churches would respond?
- Is this dilemma an issue of submission, of assertion, or—? Why?

think (continued)

pray

LIVE

what i want to discuss

What have you discovered this week that you definitely want to discuss with your small group? Write that here. Then begin your small-group discussion with these thoughts.

so what?

Use the following space to summarize what you've discovered about what you and your spouse share, and what remains solely yours. Review your Beginning Place if you need to remember where you began. How does God's truth impact the next step in your journey?

then what?

What is one practical thing you can do to apply what you've discovered? Describe how you will put this into practice. What steps will you take? Remember to think realistically; an admirable but unreachable goal is as good as no goal. Discuss your goal with your small group to further define it.

how?

Identify how you will be held accountable to the goal you described. Who will be on your support team? What are their responsibilities? How will you measure the success of your plan? Write the details here.

bed

"The messages are loud, clear, and mixed: sex is everything, sex is nothing, sex is something. But what should sex be for us? Should there even be a *should* in there? What do we want it to be, and why isn't it?"

the beginning place

Middle-aged husband, raised in the church: "Sex was supposed to be sacred—which said, to me at least, that sex wasn't as much fun as it was a sacrament."

Thirtysomething wife: "What's a Christian couple to do when, before you're married, the church's sex message is 'Don't do it, guard against it, it's sin, watch out'—and then after a half-hour ceremony, 'It's right, it's holy, go for it.' Who can *go for it* after decades of being warned against it?"

Author of a Christian sex manual: "Men, if you want to do something that your wife will find sexy and sensual, try this simple act of foreplay: Pray with her."

It all begins with sex, someone said. After all, weren't "Be fruitful and multiply" among the Creator's first recorded words? And since then the sexuality of our race has energized virtually every aspect of human culture—religion, government, education, art, finance—thrumming and pulsing just below the surface or audaciously bursting out to nakedly inspire, influence, entice.

The kings and poets and prophets who wrote the Old Testament weren't squeamish about sex. They wrote about it like it was part of the weather—sex and its results could soothe like a zephyr breeze (see the Song of Songs) or destroy like a sandstorm (the sexual escapades in just King David's family had paralyzing, long-term repercussions). The Wisdom writers of the book of Proverbs wrote of Lady Wisdom and Madame Insight, contrasting her with the Temptress, the Seductress.

Sex was an aspect of the model for Yahweh's relationship with his people: Israel was his young wife who lost no time cheating on him, sleeping around the neighborhood with every Canaanite god she could get into bed. In their first-century letters to new Christians in Asia and Europe, the apostles used this same sexual imagery, but tweaked it: The bride was no longer Israel but the followers of Christ, and the groom was specifically Jesus. And by the time you reach Revelation, you're reading about the Great Whore as well as about a wedding supper celebrating the newlywed bride church and husband Christ.

All this is to say that the Bible oozes sexuality. Which is usually not the impression you'd get from a sampling of Christian sermons. So where'd Christianity get its sexually repressed, uptight reputation?

Closer to home: Where did you get your ideas of sex—especially of sex in marriage? From your parents? From your church? From your peers? Not that any of those are particularly better or worse sources for a satisfying sexual life, but married sex tends to level out after a while. And what you do with that reality often depends on your models of comparison.

So what sexual expectations did you and your spouse bring to your marriage? Against what standard are you gauging your sex life? Are you more inclined to worry that it's not sacred enough or not lusty enough? Apart from warnings about anything but strict monogamy or celibacy, what do you believe the Bible teaches about it? Summarize your beginning place for this lesson. We'll start here and then go deeper.

read the monotony of monogamy

From the *Utne* article "Everything You Always Wanted to Know . . .," by Jeremiah Creedon[1]

Q: Are humans monogamous?

A: No, monogamy is human. It's one of many sexual strategies we practice, and seem destined to continue practicing, until we get it right. Surveys say that as many as half of all American men report having had extramarital sex at least once. The rate among women is said to be one in three, though they're also apparently more prone to fib about it.

We're not the only animals with a taste for sexual novelty. Thanks to "genetic fingerprinting" techniques that can determine parentage, researchers have found more cheating in the wild kingdom than on country-western radio. Even among species that once were thought to practice fidelity, it turns out scientists were often seeing what they wanted to see. "The pattern is painfully clear," write zoologist David P. Barash and psychiatrist Judith Eve Lipton in *The Myth of Monogamy.* "In the animal world generally, and the avian world in particular, there is a whole lot more screwing around than we had thought."

Faced with evidence that females are just as randy as males, some evolutionary biologists say "sperm competition" may be the reason. Imagine a cross between water polo and *The Bachelorette.* If sperm are seen as fighting it out among themselves for the right to fertilize an egg, it figures that females benefit (via better offspring) from having multiple partners, too.

Humans have a long history of not looking too closely at paternity, but the new genetic lie detectors may change that. As Barash and Lipton note, the "monogamous family is very definitely under siege, and not by government, not by a declining moral fiber, and certainly not by some vast homosexual agenda . . . but by the dictates of biology itself."

Hebrews 13:4

Honor marriage, and guard the sacredness of sexual intimacy between wife and husband. God draws a firm line against casual and illicit sex.

think

- Do you believe that humans are naturally monogamous, naturally polygamous, or—? Why? Does your belief square with what you observe in the world around you?
- In what ways could the biblical imperative in Hebrews support and reinforce Creedon's argument?
- Why do you suppose God puts such strict limits on our sexual behavior if we are indeed polygamous by nature?
- How does your culture encourage you to honor your marriage? How does your culture discourage it?

pray

read who's on top?

1 Corinthians 7:1-6

Now, getting down to the questions you asked in your letter to me. First, Is it a good thing to have sexual relations?

Certainly—but only within a certain context. It's good for a man to have a wife, and for a woman to have a husband. Sexual drives are strong, but marriage is strong enough to contain them and provide for a balanced and fulfilling sexual life in a world of sexual disorder. The marriage bed must be a place of mutuality—the husband seeking to satisfy his wife, the wife seeking to satisfy her husband. Marriage is not a place to "stand up for your rights." Marriage is a decision to serve the other, whether in bed or out. Abstaining from sex is permissible for a period of time if you both agree to it, and if it's for the purposes of prayer and fasting—but only for such times. Then come back together again. Satan has an ingenious way of tempting us when we least expect it. I'm not, understand, commanding these periods of abstinence—only providing my best counsel if you should choose them.

think

- What do you hear the apostle Paul saying concerning the idea of the "good old days" of widespread sexual morality? Would you say that today's world is no more sexually loose than the world has ever been? Why?
- "The marriage bed must be a place of mutuality"—how would this apostolic declaration fly in a group of your church friends? Among your colleagues at work?
- Paul wrote that marriage isn't the place to stand up for your rights. Does this mean we have no rights in marriage? Talk about this.
- Recall some "ingenious ways" Satan has tempted you in your marriage.

think (continued)

pray

read sex isn't the only thing

1 Corinthians 6:16-17

There's more to sex than mere skin on skin. Sex is as much spiritual mystery as physical fact. As written in Scripture, "The two become one." Since we want to become spiritually one with the Master, we must not pursue the kind of sex that avoids commitment and intimacy, leaving us more lonely than ever—the kind of sex that can never "become one."

From the review of *Three Colors: Red*, by Vanes Naldi and Mike Lorefice[2]

Films that are about people who are together but aren't having sex are oh so much more interesting because they have to actually do some work. . . . It's rare that a film takes the time to develop what people get from a relationship when it's neither physical nor sappy sentimental mush. . . . Sex isn't the only thing you need from the opposite sex, and Valentine and The Judge both get what they need out of their relationship with one another. They gain a great friend that they can be completely honest with. That might be less fun than a lover, but it's much more valuable because it's far rarer.

think

- If you could get the film reviewer and the apostle in the same room, what do you suppose they could agree about? What would they disagree about?
- Have you ever felt that sex actually gets in the way of an interesting and honest relationship? Talk about this.
- What vision or ideal from these two quotes could be distilled into a goal for your marriage?

think (continued)

pray

read the bible says what?

From *Becoming a Couple of Promise*, by Kevin Leman[3]

What do the Scriptures say about sex? Take this true or false test.

____ 1. God cares about who's in bed with us.

____ 2. In summing up the Genesis model of marriage, Jesus referred to sexual intercourse.

____ 3. According to the Bible, sex is only for procreation, not for pleasure.

____ 4. Far from viewing sex as a divine concession to our human frailty, the Scriptures *urge* spouses to have sex (calling it a duty).

____ 5. From the beginning, the man wasn't a "finished product" without the woman.

____ 6. The Bible recommends long periods of sexual abstinence in a marriage for deeper spiritual growth and maturity.

____ 7. Male and female sexuality expresses divine creativity and says something about what God is like.

____ 8. Red-hot sexual passion is celebrated in the Bible.

____ 9. A husband has complete control and discretion over his own body, and the same is true of a wife.

____ 10. The Bible prefers that we keep bodily sensations strictly regulated, as much as possible, calling us to a purely "spiritual" life instead.

Answers on page 73.

Need clues? Read these Bible passages:

Genesis 1:27
Genesis 2:18-23
Proverbs 5:18-19

Song of Songs 4:9–5:5
Mark 10:7-8
1 Corinthians 7:3
1 Corinthians 7:4-5
Colossians 2:20-23
Hebrews 13:4

think

- Anything surprising in these questions or answers? If so, what? If no, why not?
- How would you respond to someone who said, "Read the Bible cold, at face value, and you'll find precious little prudery or Puritanism. Whatever shame is associated with sexuality among some Christians has been merely tacked onto an otherwise lusty and full-bodied Christianity"?
- If many beliefs widely held to be biblical actually aren't—that sex is primarily for procreation, not pleasure, for example, or that God is a little embarrassed by red-hot sex among humans—where did those beliefs come from?

think (continued)

The false statements are

3 (*see Proverbs 5:18-19*)

6 (*see 1 Corinthians 7:5*)

9 (*see 1 Corinthians 7:4*)

10 (*see Colossians 2:20-23*)

pray

read bringing lust home

From the *Psychotherapy Networker* article "In Search of Erotic Intelligence: Reconciling Sensuality and Domesticity," by Esther Perel[4]

Terry had been in therapy for a year, struggling with the transition from being half of an erotically charged couple to being one-quarter of a family with two children and no eroticism at all. He began one session with what he deemed a "real midlife story" that began when he and his wife hired a young German au pair. "Every morning she and I take care of my daughters together," he said, "She's lovely—so natural, full of vitality and youth—and I've developed this amazing crush on her. You know how I've been talking about this feeling of deadness? Well, her energy has awakened me. I want to sleep with her and I wonder why I don't. I'm scared to do it and scared not to."

I didn't lecture him about his "immature" wishes, or explore the emotional dynamics beneath this presumably "adolescent" desire. Instead, I tried to help him relish the awakening of his dormant senses without letting the momentary exhilaration endanger his marriage. I marveled with him at the allure and beauty of fantasy, while also calling it just that: a *fantasy.*

"It's great to know you still can come to life like that," I said. "And you know that you can never compare this state of inebriation with life at home, because home is shaky ground, you like it, but you're also afraid that it can take you too far away from home. And you probably don't let your wife evoke such tremors in you."

A few days later, he was having lunch in a restaurant with his wife and she was telling him of her previous boyfriend. "I'd been thinking hard about what we talked about," he told me, "and at the table I had this switch. Normally, I don't like hearing these stories of hers—they make me jealous and irritated. But this time I just listened and found myself getting very turned on. So did she. In fact, we were so excited we had to look for a bathroom where we could be alone."

I suggested that perhaps the experience of desiring a fresh young woman was what enabled him to listen to his wife differently—as a sexual and desirable woman herself. I invited Terry to permit himself the erotic intensity of the illicit with his wife: "This could be a beginning of bringing lust home," I said. "These small transgressions are acceptable; they offer you the latitude to experience new desire without having to throw everything away."

It amazes me how willing people are to experiment sexually *outside* their relationships, yet how tame and puritanical they are with their partners. . . .

A fundamental conundrum is that we seek a steady, reliable anchor in our partner, at the same time we seek a transcendent experience that allows us to soar beyond our ordinary lives. The challenge, then for couples and therapist, is to reconcile the need for what's safe and predictable with the wish to pursue what's exciting, mysterious, and awe-inspiring.

think

- According to the author, couples need to reconcile "what's safe and predictable with . . . what's exciting, mysterious, and awe-inspiring." Talk about this.
- Are infatuations and crushes on people other than your spouse inevitable? If not, how do you avoid them? If so, how do you defuse them?
- What do you think about the idea of bringing home erotic intensity to your spouse?
- Spend some time talking with your spouse about the previous question. Remember, communicate!

think (continued)

pray

read those hot hebrews

Veteran rocker David Bowie[5]

> You Americans. I think there is a fundamental Puritanism in most of the exploits of the Americans, and I think it carries through to their pleasure pursuits, as well. Europeans are perverse; we're a very old, decadent culture. We like things kind of messed up. . . . There is an openness that is not genre-oriented. That sort of thing doesn't come easily for Americans.

Song of Songs 1:2-4,12-13,16; 4:2-6

[Her:]
Kiss me—full on the mouth!
    Yes! For your love is better than wine,
    headier than your aromatic oils.
The syllables of your name murmur like a meadow brook.
    No wonder everyone loves to say your name!

Take me away with you! Let's run off together!
    An elopement with my King-Lover!
    We'll celebrate, we'll sing,
    we'll make great music.
Yes! For your love is better than vintage wine. . . .

When my King-Lover lay down beside me,
    my fragrance filled the room.
His head resting between my breasts—
    the head of my lover was a sachet of sweet myrrh. . . .

And you, my dear lover—you're so handsome!
    And the bed we share is like a forest glen. . . .

[Him:]
Your smile is generous and full—
    expressive and strong and clean.
Your lips are jewel red,
    your mouth elegant and inviting,
    your veiled cheeks soft and radiant.
The smooth, lithe lines of your neck
    command notice—all heads turn in awe and admiration!
Your breasts are like fawns,
    twins of a gazelle, grazing among the first spring flowers.

The sweet, fragrant curves of your body,
    the soft, spiced contours of your flesh
Invite me, and I come. I stay
    until dawn breathes its light and night slips away.

think

- What about Bowie's observation strikes you as accurate? Inaccurate?
- How do you suppose Bowie would respond to the Song of Songs?
- How do you respond to it? Does it seem in the same key, so to speak, as the rest of the Bible's teachings on marriage, or in another key altogether?
- In light of such biblical passages, how could your marriage provide a contrast to Christianity's reputation for repressed sexuality?

think (continued)

pray

LIVE

what i want to discuss

What have you discovered this week that you definitely want to discuss with your small group? Write that here. Then begin your small-group discussion with these thoughts.

so what?

Use the following space to summarize what you've discovered during this chapter about sex in your marriage. Review your Beginning Place if you need to remember where you began. How does God's truth impact the next step in your journey?

then what?

What is one practical thing you can do to apply what you've discovered? Describe how you will put this into practice. What steps will you take? Remember to think realistically; an admirable but unreachable goal is as good as no goal. Discuss your goal with your small group to further define it.

how?

Identify how you will be held accountable to the goal you described. Who will be on your support team? What are their responsibilities? How will you measure the success of your plan? Write the details here.

ghosts

"My father isn't here, but I sense that he dominates this marriage. I don't like it, but I don't know how to shake it off."

the beginning place

Both of them were Christians from early childhood. Neither could remember a time they didn't dress up and pile into their respective station wagons each week and head for Sunday school. The two of them first met in their church's youth group, which became their social circle throughout high school. She was the pastor's daughter, he was the youth group president and, later, a Christian college graduate. They were raised in the same denomination, they embraced the same moral values, and they were unified in their beliefs. Their engagement and subsequent marriage was a natural. A perfect match. A union of two like-minded Christians determined to serve God together.

Yet every marriage is a mixed marriage, as more than one person has observed. And it took this couple fifteen years and a tanked marriage that somehow survived to realize that, for all their similarities, just under the surface one of them might as well have been a suave Viennese agnostic and the other an Amazonian animist. You would never have detected much difference between them by comparing written statements of faith. Yet a closer look at fundamental perceptions—their deep images of God, their expectations of humanity, their perceptions of self, their read on why stuff happens in this life—revealed significant differences in their emotional and spiritual landscapes. And not recognizing or acknowledging these profound differences early in their relationship contributed to a lot of agony later on.

You may remember the bedroom scene in the movie *The Story of Us*, in which Ben and Katie (Bruce Willis and Michelle Pfeiffer) try to talk themselves through a difficult patch in their marriage—and joining them in bed are the palpable presences of their four parents. It is a vivid reminder that even in bed you escape neither your parents nor your spouse's parents.

It cuts both ways, though: what we grew up observing and experiencing as children, then consciously or unconsciously brought into a marriage—it has as much blessing as baggage. Indeed, are we not exhorted to teach our children well in order to prepare them for adulthood, for marriage, for real life? Alas, if only we could limit our lessons to only healthy lessons.

So what ancestral habits and attitudes have you brought into your marriage? How long did it take you to recognize them? Which attitudes have helped your marriage, and which have hindered it? Use the space below to summarize your beginning place for this lesson. Describe to what degree you sense yourself living out the behaviors of your forebears, and its effect on you and your spouse. We'll start here and then go deeper.

read our ancestors live in us

From the *ASU Research* article "A Woman's Place," by Laura Tohe[1]

> I was raised among storytellers. I am very much influenced by hearing the stories of my family, of my ancestors, and of Navajo beliefs. . . .
>
> A story is our umbilical cord to the past. The experiences of our ancestors influence, in many ways, who we are and the choices we make. Those experiences, those stories, are always being repeated. So, if you don't know those stories, then you're at a loss. You're an empty person.

think

- Tell a story from an earlier generation in your family that is "an umbilical cord"—a story that ties you to your past.
- What of you does that story contain?
- Has this story—or any other family story you've heard—influenced who you are or any choices you've made, at least that you're conscious of?
- If your extended family is rich in stories, try to imagine what it would be like growing up without them. If intergenerational stories are rare in your family, why do you suppose that is? What do you think you're missing by the absence of family stories?

pray

read you marry the child

From *Becoming a Couple of Promise*, by Kevin Leman[2]

Some of you are, indeed, paying for your mate's background, upbringing, past disappointments, and failures. That's because of a simple principle that many of us never discover until after we say our vows: *You date the adult; you marry the child.*

Yes, you marry the child your spouse once was. If I were to put my little girl on a ladder, moving her higher and higher up the rungs to a height of twenty feet, she'd jump to me. I would catch her, too. She knows that and jumps to me. In some cases, though, when a little child has done a swan dive, the other person has pulled back. So the child shuts down from that point on, not wanting to risk trusting others again. You, as the spouse, are then forced to live with the consequences of that early crisis. . . .

If husbands and wives want to trace some important parental influences, they need to look at four family relationships:

- How Dad treated Mom
- How Mom treated Dad
- How Dad treated the daughter
- How Mom treated the son

When Dad treated Mom badly, for example, the repercussions can pop up years later after the children are grown. Just being aware of how you were parented (including all the dynamics of the relationship between you and your parents) can be a tremendous advantage.

think

- Try to recall the moment when you first glimpsed an unknown emotional territory in your spouse.
- How are you, in Leman's words, "paying for your mate's background, upbringing, past disappointments, and failures"?

- On a scale of 1 to 10 (1 being oblivious, 10 being excruciatingly aware), how conscious are you of the connection between how you were parented and the kind of spouse you are?

pray

read chip off the old block

Genesis 12:10-20; 20:1-15; 26:6-11

Then a famine came to the land. Abram went down to Egypt to live; it was a hard famine. As he drew near to Egypt, he said to his wife, Sarai, "Look. We both know that you're a beautiful woman. When the Egyptians see you they're going to say, "Aha! That's his wife!' and kill me. But they'll let you live. Do me a favor: tell them you're my sister. Because of you, they'll welcome me and let me live."

When Abram arrived in Egypt, the Egyptians took one look and saw that his wife was stunningly beautiful. Pharaoh's princes raved over her to Pharaoh. She was taken to live with Pharaoh.

Because of her, Abram got along very well: he accumulated sheep and cattle, male and female donkeys, men and women servants, and camels. But GOD hit Pharaoh hard because of Abram's wife Sarai; everybody in the palace got seriously sick.

Pharaoh called for Abram, "What's this that you've done to me? Why didn't you tell me that she's your wife? Why did you say, 'She's my sister' so that I'd take her as my wife? Here's your wife back—take her and get out!"

Pharaoh ordered his men to get Abram out of the country. They sent him and his wife and everything he owned on their way.

[Later in their marriage . . .]
Abraham traveled from [the Oaks of Mamre] south to the Negev and settled down between Kadesh and Shur. While he was camping in Gerar, Abraham said of his wife Sarah, "She's my sister."

So Abimelech, king of Gerar, sent for Sarah and took her. But God came to Abimelech in a dream that night and told him, "You're as good as dead—that woman you took, she's a married woman."

Now Abimelech had not yet slept with her, hadn't so much as touched her. He said, "Master, would you kill an innocent man? Didn't he tell me, 'She's my sister'? And didn't she herself say, 'He's my brother'? I had no idea I was doing anything wrong when I did this."

God said to him in the dream, "Yes, I know your intentions were pure, that's why I kept you from sinning against me; I was the one who kept you from going to bed with her. So now give the man's wife back to him. He's a prophet and will pray for you—pray for your life. If you don't give her back, know that it's certain death both for you and everyone in your family."

Abimelech was up first thing in the morning. He called all his house servants together and told them the whole story. They were shocked. Then Abimelech called in Abraham and said, "What have you done to us? What have I ever done to you that you would bring on me and my kingdom this huge offense? What you've done to me ought never to have been done."

Abimelech went on to Abraham, "Whatever were you thinking of when you did this thing?"

Abraham said, "I just assumed that there was no fear of God in this place and that they'd kill me to get my wife. Besides, the truth is that she is my half sister; she's my father's daughter but not my mother's. When God sent me out as a wanderer from my father's home, I told her, 'Do me a favor; wherever we go, tell people that I'm your brother.'"

Then Abimelech gave Sarah back to Abraham, and along with her sent sheep and cattle and servants, both male and female. He said, "My land is open to you; live wherever you wish."

[And a generation later . . .]
So Isaac [the son of Abraham] stayed put in Gerar.

The men of the place questioned him about his wife. He said, "She's my sister." He was afraid to say, "She's my wife." He was thinking, "These men might kill me to get Rebekah, she's so beautiful."

One day, after they had been there quite a long time, Abimelech, king of the Philistines, looked out his window and saw Isaac fondling his wife Rebekah. Abimelech sent for Isaac and said, "So, she's your wife. Why did you tell us 'She's my sister'?"

Isaac said, "Because I thought I might get killed by someone who wanted her."

Abimelech said, "But think of what you might have done to *us*! Given a little more time, one of the men might have slept with your wife; you would have been responsible for bringing guilt down on us."

Then Abimelech gave orders to his people: "Anyone who so much as lays a hand on this man or his wife dies."

think

- What surprised you in these passages?
- What do these narratives tell you about Abraham and Isaac?
- Could there be a brighter side to these humiliating incidents? Can you read anything healthy between the lines that Isaac inherited from his dad?
- Name a dark tendency you inherited from your father, one that surfaces often in your marriage.
- Now name a strength you inherited from your father, one that graces your marriage.

pray

read the classic mother-to-wife transfer

From *Intimate Partners: Patterns in Love and Marriage*, by Maggie Scarf[3]

"There's something from the past here," I found myself speaking aloud, "and it's almost a sense of being dependent on a person whom you don't really want to be linked up with. Is that something that rings a bell for you from a time when you were a young child—say, seven, eight or thereabouts?"

He looked at me as if I'd asked him a question in a language he didn't understand.

"Was there a problem, in terms of your not feeling the things you were supposed to feel for your mother? For instance, did you love her enough?"

Gordon opened his mouth, but said nothing, for the carillon of the Harkness Tower bells suddenly commanded the attention of the world around. In the wake of their melody, his voice was sober. "I can remember getting strange messages from my mother. Like 'If you weren't adopted, where would you be?' And those, not unreasonably, were interpreted as 'I must not be a good person' or 'I must be doing something wrong.'" His voice was no longer angry-sounding. He sounded dispirited or even depressed.

He had, he said suddenly, tried very hard to please.

"You tried hard to please?" I repeated his words. He nodded. "Yes, and I never felt that I was doing quite well enough at it."

He had had, as a child, the "wrong caretaker," and—since he himself did not have the right feelings about her—his survival in that situation was precarious. For if he didn't really love his mother, she might realize it and respond by not caring for *him.* He was, moreover, undoubtedly not only fearful but deeply guilty about his true feelings toward his parent. Now, the same things were happening in the present situation with the new caretaker who was his spouse.

How often, in the dawn of life, are we presented with certain kinds of problems which we attempt to re-create and to work upon, subsequently, with our mates? We seem to be uncannily *efficient* when it comes to choosing partners who will help us get into situations that recapitulate earlier dilemmas that have never been successfully mastered. It is as if we were guided by a dizzyingly complex and yet remarkably precise internalized radar.

"There are elements of my mother's personality in Jo Ann," observed Gordon. "I guess a lot of that dependability and nursing . . . She is solid, and you know she will be there; she won't run out doing flighty things." The early, frustrating relationship with his adoptive mother had been replicated in the present, frustrating situation with his wife. He himself could not be in any *other* kind of marital system, for this was the only kind of intimate relationship that he really knew about—one in which he felt dependent for nurturance upon a person for whom he did not have the correctly affectionate feelings.

think

- You've been given permission to ask either Gordon or Jo Ann one question. What would it be?
- If you are a husband, what about your mother have you been aware of subtly transferring to your wife? If you're not aware of anything, just ponder this awhile.
- If you are a wife, what about your father have you been aware of subtly transferring to your husband? Again, if nothing comes to mind, just stay with the question for a moment.
- Do you agree or disagree with the author's belief that we seem to choose a spouse with whom we "recapitulate earlier dilemmas that have never been successfully mastered"? Why do you think so?
- If Scarf is correct, what could be the hopefulness within this apparent frustration?

think (continued)

pray

read you're on your own

Ezekiel 18:1-4,14-17,19-20

GOD'S Message to me: "What do you people mean by going around the country repeating the saying,

The parents ate green apples,
The children got stomachache?

"As sure as I'm the living God, you're not going to repeat this saying in Israel any longer. Every soul—man, woman, child—belongs to me, parent and child alike. You die for your own sin, not another's. . . .

"Now look: Suppose that this child has a child who sees all the sins done by his parent. The child sees them, but doesn't follow in the parent's footsteps—

doesn't eat at the pagan shrines,
doesn't worship the popular idols of Israel,
doesn't seduce his neighbor's spouse,
doesn't bully anyone,
doesn't refuse to loan money,
doesn't steal,
doesn't refuse food to the hungry,
doesn't refuse to give clothes to the ill-clad,
doesn't live by impulse and greed,
doesn't exploit the poor.
He does what I say;
he performs my laws and lives by my statutes.

"This person will not die for the sins of the parent; he will live truly and well. . . .

"Do you need to ask, 'So why does the child not share the guilt of the parent?'

"Isn't it plain? It's because the child did what is fair and right. Since the child was careful to do what is lawful and right, the child will live truly and well. The soul that sins is the soul that dies. The child does not share the guilt of the parent, nor the parent the guilt of the child."

think

- Do your best to come up with a modern equivalent for the ancient adage "The parents ate green apples, the children got stomachache."
- How does the prophet's tirade here compare with modern thought about influences between parents and children?
- Does what you know of the Bible make you think it leans toward "Everyone is responsible for making their own decisions"? Or toward "There are influences prodding you at every turn of your life"?
- If you were to apply this prophetic passage to your marriage, what would it sound like (in one sentence)?

pray

read it need not be your destiny

From *The Sacred Journey: A Memoir of Early Days*, by Frederick Buechner[4]

When somebody answered the phone, I asked to speak to my uncle, and there was a clumsy silence at the other end of the line. Then his son and namesake, my cousin and childhood friend, came on and told me that early that morning, before anybody was up, his father had walked out of his bedroom into the next room and shot himself.

When the river slows down at a bend or deepens, currents from below wrinkle the silken surface and, if a leaf drifts by, catch it and spin it around and around and around; and if the current is strong enough, the leaf is sucked under, or if the leaf is lucky enough, it spins free and continues downstream into the swift white water beyond. It was the sheer melodrama of it that spun me around first—one brother [Buechner's own father also killed himself, years earlier], then another brother, like a family curse to be handed down from one generation to the next till some ancient, unknown wrong was righted at last. . . .

When it got into the newspapers, I felt myself expected to play some sort of tragic role that in a way I had no true heart for. What might have sucked me under was not the grief but the fear of it—the fear that there might really be some fatal family flaw that I had inherited like the cut of my jaw or that, by some grim process of autosuggestion if nothing else, I would end up as those two brothers had. . . . In any case, I spun free of the dark eddy. . . . It was by grace of nothing more if nothing less than sheer earthly delight in the gift to me of the earth and of my own life under the sun and moon that I was carried past the dangerous, downward pull of my uncle's death.

think

- Does it sound to you like it was God or simply the luck of the draw that saved him from the black eddy of despair? Or—?
- Was there ever a time in your life—or in the life of someone close to you—when, against a backdrop and even premonition of tragedy, you (or another) beat the odds and walked away from what looked like inevitable emotional or spiritual disaster?
- What variables have to line up if your marriage is going to be decisively influenced by your familial past? And conversely, what details might make for a weak influence of your ancestors on you and your marriage?

pray

LIVE

what i want to discuss

What have you discovered this week that you definitely want to discuss with your small group? Write that here. Then begin your small-group discussion with these thoughts.

so what?

Use the following space to summarize what you've discovered during this chapter about the influence of family members on your marriage. Review your Beginning Place if you need to remember where you began. How does God's truth impact the next step in your journey?

then what?

What is one practical thing you can do to apply what you've discovered? Describe how you will put this into practice. What steps will you take? Remember to think realistically; an admirable but unreachable goal is as good as no goal. Discuss your goal with your small group to further define it.

how?

Identify how you will be held accountable to the goal you described. Who will be on your support team? What are their responsibilities? How will you measure the success of your plan? Write the details here.

children

"I miss that just-us-two feeling we had before kids came along.
I feel like I lost my partner then, and I haven't gotten him back yet."

the beginning place

You've seen your thirteen-year-old change a lot in the last couple of years. You've been told—and perhaps observed some of it, if not as a parent—that children of the West have changed over the last century. Now add to these changes how the significance of children has changed to what we see today.

There were some blips and anomalies along the way, but until recently, children were conceived frequently, often died young, and were assigned domestic duties as early as possible. Class and status added some variations, with children of the affluent being passed off to a wet nurse upon birth, then to a nanny, and typically spared the grueling childhood of the masses.

As part of a family, children plowed, wove, cooked, herded—whatever they could do to keep the family fed, clothed, sheltered; in short, kids were financial assets. They were also evidence of virility and fertility, an initiation for their mothers into full womanhood, the source of their parents' social fulfillment, and evidence of divine approval.

Children born into the Industrial Revolution kept on working hard—but as employees for poverty-level wages instead of on their parents' land. Instead of working side by side with siblings or parents, kids chiseled coal in mines, sweated out fifty-six-hour workweeks in mills, and hustled for whatever pittance they could add to the family income.

During the last century, however, the American farm family has faded away, resulting in less and less actual need for children. As a result, children ceased being their parents' social fulfillment, becoming instead a purely sentimental, emotional, or spiritual fulfillment.

Financially speaking, kids have become an unmitigated liability. (Babycenter.com/costofchild is an online calculator that—with figures from the U.S. Department of Agriculture—churns out what you will pay for your bundle of joy's first eighteen years: Given two parents, a modest household income, and four years at a public university, you'll dish out $400,000 to $450,000.)

And as much as children remain a kind of fulfillment of marriage, they are at the same time an imposition on it. Talk to most couples, and you'll hear about the wedges that children drive between their parents. They're darling, of course, veritable godsends, cute, and full of potential—yet over the course of five or ten years they can reduce a pair of adult lovers into cohabiting strangers.

And yet we keep having them, feeding them, loving them, doing our best to raise them. We see ourselves in our children, ourselves with a do-over on life, and want them to surpass us in every way.

So what do you see at the intersection of your marriage and your children? If you're still in the planning stages, how do you imagine it? What about child rearing are you breezing through, and what about it absolutely blindsided you and your spouse? How are you coping? And how is the marriage faring through it all? Summarize your beginning place for this lesson. Describe your experience in juggling children with your mate, how you think your marriage has influenced your parenting, and how your parenting has affected your marriage. We'll start here and then go deeper.

read best gift to children

From *Two-Part Invention: The Story of a Marriage,* by Madeleine L'Engle[1]

> One time after I had given a talk to a large library-association annual meeting, one of the librarians asked me, "What do you think you and Hugh do that is best for your children?"
>
> And I answered off the top of my head, "We love each other."
>
> And I'm sure that *is* the best thing we could possibly have given them. But in being lovers, in being parents, we have had to take risks. We have had to be open to crisis.

think

- Does L'Engle's answer strike you more as simplistic or profound? Why?
- Is it impossible for parents to love each other to the neglect of their children? Why?
- If you are married with children, when have you noticed that an improvement in your marriage also improved something about your kids?
- Under what circumstances do you think that a marriage might sometimes have to be put on hold while the parents' attention is directed solely to the kids?

pray

read string that bow!

Psalm 127:3-5

Don't you see that children are GOD's best gift?
  the fruit of the womb his generous legacy?
Like a warrior's fistful of arrows
  are the children of a vigorous youth.
Oh, how blessed are you parents,
  with your quivers full of children!
Your enemies don't stand a chance against you;
  you'll sweep them right off your doorstep.

think

- Here it is—the classic biblical passage that compares a houseful of children to a quiver full of arrows. How does that comparison sit with you?
- If you were to modernize the comparison—since today's culture doesn't have much use for bows and arrows—how would you update the metaphor?
- That children can be a joy and a comfort is common knowledge. Yet how could your children defend you against enemies? Let this one simmer awhile.
- What do you make of the psalmist's claim in the first line—that children are God's best gift? Might the psalmist have been a little carried away and exaggerated the benefit of children? Or do you think the psalmist is right on? Why?

think (continued)

pray

read us edged out by them

From *The Shelter of Each Other*, by Mary Pipher[2]

Edwardo said, "We are here to make our marriage better. We don't believe in divorce."

"Besides," Sabrina added, "we've cared about each other since the day we met."

Edwardo smiled. "We met at a high school track meet. I was attracted to Sabrina's hurdle jumping."

Sabrina laughed. "You were attracted to my body, admit it."

They dated for a year and married young. The twins were an expensive surprise. Since the boys' birth, life had been tough. Edwardo and Sabrina cared for each other, but they had definitely fallen out of love. Edwardo said, "I know my problems at work aren't Sabrina's fault, but sometimes I take my anger out on her." Sabrina said, "We almost never see each other, and when we do we argue about who is going to take down the trash or bathe the twins."

"If you could stay up past nine, we might have more of a relationship," Edwardo said. Sabrina nodded miserably and explained that she was always tired. At Kmart she supervised twenty-six checkers. She was on her feet all day, dealing with disgruntled customers, spills, returns and broken scanners. Some days she had time to wolf down a corn dog or taco, other days she worked through the lunch hour. At five, she managed to get out of there and into rush-hour traffic. She picked up the boys, who were fussy and tired. Lately the day-care operator complained that Jorge might be hyperactive. He hit other kids and drove the caregivers crazy. Sabrina was worried that the woman would kick the twins out. The Jolly Tots wasn't great, but they could afford it. Sabrina knew the boys were physically safe, if not terribly well entertained or cared for, and there weren't other options.

think

- Do you think Edwardo and Sabrina's situation is common or uncommon? Why?
- How is your experience similar to and different from Edwardo and Sabrina's?
- If you were the counselor in the room, what direction would you explore with them? What questions would you ask?
- If you've ever been in circumstances similar to these, how did you emerge from them? Or did you?

pray

read the very essence of the kingdom

Matthew 18:1-5

At about the same time, the disciples came to Jesus asking, "Who gets the highest rank in God's kingdom?"

For an answer Jesus called over a child, whom he stood in the middle of the room, and said, "I'm telling you, once and for all, that unless you return to square one and start over like children, you're not even going to get a look at the kingdom, let alone get in. Whoever becomes simple and elemental again, like this child, will rank high in God's kingdom. What's more, when you receive the childlike on my account, it's the same as receiving me."

Mark 10:13-16

The people brought children to Jesus, hoping he might touch them. The disciples shooed them off. But Jesus was irate and let them know it: "Don't push these children away. Don't ever get between them and me. These children are at the very center of life in the kingdom. Mark this: Unless you accept God's kingdom in the simplicity of a child, you'll never get in." Then, gathering the children up in his arms, he laid his hands of blessing on them.

think

- Do you think "children are at the very center of life in the kingdom"? Why? Do you see this in everyday life?
- How literal do you think Jesus was being when he said that receiving the childlike on his account is the same as receiving him?
- What are some implications for a marriage if children are as fundamentally significant to spirituality as Jesus said they were?
- What would be your response if someone said, "If children are as central to spiritual life as Jesus said they were, why didn't he have any?"

think (continued)

pray

read friendly territory

From the *Washington Post* article "Branson, Mo., Looks Beyond RVs and Buffets: Prosperous Conservative Movement Has Blue-Collar Retreat Aiming to Go Upscale," by Lois Romano[3]

> For David and Melissa Egli of Fort Dodge, Iowa—first-time visitors [to Branson, Missouri] with their six children—the Christian themes and family-friendly atmosphere will bring them back.
>
> "It's a draw for us . . . very important," said Melissa Egli, 34, who home-schools her children. "Any more you're made to feel uncomfortable being a Christian."
>
> David Egli works for the railroads, so the family is able to travel around the country for minimal cost. But they have found that "larger cities are almost hostile to large families," he said. "You sit down with six kids, and it's like they roll their eyes."
>
> In Branson, Egli said, "it's like birds of a feather flock together. Christian families are getting larger and larger, taking the biblical approach in trusting God for the number of children. . . . Here, we found a lot of people like us. We found a place where we connected."

think

- How did having children affect David and Melissa's marriage?
- How has having children (if you have them) affected your faith and how you express it?
- In what sense have you, like the Eglis, been drawn, like "birds of a feather," to families just like yours? In what sense have you sought the company of families different from yours?
- How would you have connected with other people or other kinds of people if you didn't have kids? Talk about this.

think (continued)

pray

read influence cuts both ways

From *Raising Adults: Getting Kids Ready for the Real World*, by Jim Hancock[4]

> We regale them with stories about how things were different when we were young. We burned with purpose and passion; we *did* something when we were young. We did something about civil rights and the war—*The War*: our muddy, bloody skirmishes in the Mekong Delta or the Gulf of Tonkin or Kent State or Chicago. And for the most part they listen politely, or at least they don't say much. But they wonder what happened to the fire.
>
> How could we be so vital and alive back then and so dull and workaday now? How could we trade passion for a European car? Sure, we elected a president who's our age and just like us. So what? What have we done lately, *personally*, to make the world better?
>
> "Adults no longer behave like adults," says a 22-year-old female. "We have no role models; they're talking about sex and therapy and substance abuse, just like us."

think

- Consider this: Your marriage is not only influenced by children, but can be a potent influencer of them, too. List one way your marriage could make the world better for all children within your sphere of influence.
- Now list two more ways your marriage could improve the world of your children.
- Evaluate the indictment that "adults no longer behave like adults." Assume the young woman's voice and complete this sentence: An ideal adult is ____________________________.
- What pressures and stresses do you experience that your parents didn't have? Could that explain why today's parents seem so unheroic?

think (continued)

pray

LIVE

what i want to discuss

What have you discovered this week that you definitely want to discuss with your small group? Write that here. Then begin your small-group discussion with these thoughts.

so what?

Use the following space to summarize what you've discovered during this chapter about the intersection of your children and your marriage. Review your Beginning Place if you need to remember where you began. How does God's truth impact the next step in your journey?

then what?

What is one practical thing you can do to apply what you've discovered? Describe how you will put this into practice. What steps will you take? Remember to think realistically; an admirable but unreachable goal is as good as no goal. Discuss your goal with your small group to further define it.

how?

Identify how you will be held accountable to the goal you described. Who will be on your support team? What are their responsibilities? How will you measure the success of your plan? Write the details here.

again

"I don't have to be told how dicey a second or third marriage is. But really, this time I want to do it right."

the beginning place

"Marriage," said one comic, "is the triumph of imagination over intelligence. Remarriage is the triumph of hope over experience."

If marriage is statistically risky, remarriages are even riskier, which explains an increased incidence—in the U.S., at least—of cohabitation following an ended marriage. Who wants to put oneself through all that again? Especially if a divorced woman agrees with that acidic cultural observer H. L. Mencken, who claimed that "once a woman passes a certain point in intelligence it is almost impossible to get a husband: she simply cannot go on listening [to men] without snickering."

Yet not all "exes" are cynics. They may date too soon, too late, too cautiously, too impulsively, too casually, too calculatingly—but date they do. And despite the finger-wagging experts who warn us that second marriages are twice as likely to dissolve as first marriages, we remarry anyway. The longing for companionship, for sex, for protection, for meaning, for romance—these are such deeply human desires that one denies them only with great self-discipline.

Interestingly enough, the apostle Paul doesn't come down clearly on one side or the other of this dilemma. In his first letter to the Corinthian Christians, chapter 7, he instructs married couples to stay married. At the same time, he suggests to unmarried readers that "singleness might well be the best thing for them"—unless, that is, "they can't manage their desires and emotions." In that case he says to "go ahead and get married. The difficulties of marriage are preferable by far to a sexually tortured life as a single."

What's a twenty-first-century Christian who wants to remarry to do? Preparation helps here as it does at the onset of a first marriage. And you'd think that just the life experiences of one marriage behind them would make spouses in second marriages wiser. But many spouses drag the same habits, attitudes, and assumptions that undercut their first marriages right into their second.

So how do diligent divorcees think about remarriages that will be stable and strong and satisfying? What if their churches are less than encouraging? What if a remarriage involves blending two families? ("From the teenager's perspective," writes Laurence Steinberg in *You and Your Adolescent*, "remarriage can feel like a hostile takeover.") Use the space below to summarize your beginning place for this lesson. Describe the reasons you divorced and what prompts (or prompted) you to consider another marriage. We'll start here and then go deeper.

If divorce and remarriage have not affected you directly, odds are they have indirectly. This is one of the chapters where the emphasis may not be on your marriage, but on someone else's. If you don't have anything to add to the discussion, fine. Just remember that your presence and listening ear may speak volumes of encouragement and affirmation to those beginning "again."

read just enlarging your family, or the silent treatment?

From *The Romance of the Word: One Man's Love Affair with Theology*, by Robert Farrar Capon[1]

> Perhaps [my book's] best insight is its refusal to give houseroom to the words "ex-wife" and "ex-husband." No marriages ever really end—not even the marriages of those who think they do. We simply go on adding more relationships to our already cluttered lives. We do not chuck one wife or husband for another, any more than we get rid of children in favor of stepchildren. I now have two wives and eight children—and such affinities with each of them as I can manage to muddle through. If we cannot (for all their faults and ours) have ex-parents, there is no sense in trying to "ex" anyone else out of our lives.

From *How to Be First in a Second Marriage*, by Rose Sweet[2]

> You can remain kind and courteous to your ex-wife, but you should keep communication and contact to a minimum and on a business level. This may sound pretty cold, but it is the best approach when there's continued hostility, manipulation or efforts at rekindling old roles. Spouses who continue sharing deep feelings and emotions, even negative ones, are still being "intimate" with each other.

think

- Which perspective resonates most with you? Why?
- Based on your experience or the experience of one close to you, do you agree with Capon that "no marriages ever really end"? Why?

- Why do you suppose our culture permits ex-wives and ex-husbands but generally not ex-parents?
- Compare the two authors' approaches on the basis of practicality. Do you believe it would be simpler and more efficient to recognize a continuing relationship with an ex or to reduce communication to a minimum? Why?

pray

read as usual, he keeps it simple

John 8:1-11

Jesus went across to Mount Olives, but he was soon back in the Temple again. Swarms of people came to him. He sat down and taught them.

The religion scholars and Pharisees led in a woman who had been caught in an act of adultery. They stood her in plain sight of everyone and said, "Teacher, this woman was caught red-handed in the act of adultery. Moses, in the Law, gives orders to stone such persons. What do you say?" They were trying to trap him into saying something incriminating so they could bring charges against him.

Jesus bent down and wrote with his finger in the dirt. They kept at him, badgering him. He straightened up and said, "The sinless one among you, go first: Throw the stone." Bending down again, he wrote some more in the dirt.

Hearing that, they walked away, one after another, beginning with the oldest. The woman was left alone. Jesus stood up and spoke to her. "Woman, where are they? Does no one condemn you?"

"No one, Master."

"Neither do I," said Jesus. "Go on your way. From now on, don't sin."

think

- Go ahead and add your guess to centuries of speculation: What do you think Jesus wrote with his finger in the dirt? Why?
- What do you think of the way Jesus handled the situation? What would you have done differently?
- In your experience, is Jesus' simple example followed among believers? Why?

- If you're starting over in a relationship, what do you think Jesus requires of you? What do you think your family, friends, or church requires of you? Talk about this.

pray

read fresh start for a used person

From *I Married You*, by Walter Trobisch[3]

A detailed description of her life story followed. It was as I had thought: [Fatma] was constantly searching for a place without ever finding one. When her father refused to let her marry her first suitor, she eloped with him far away from her home village. Her father tried to get her to return home, but she stubbornly refused. The legal status of her relationship to this man was not quite clear. She put it this way: "I got married to him by myself without God." After she had lived with him for some months she discovered that he already had a child with another woman. In the meantime, she was pregnant and did not dare to leave him. . . .

Finally she left the man, but he kept her son. She chased from village to village, town to town, always looking for a place, until she ended up in this city. She couldn't even remember all the men she had lived with before John took her in.

The letter ended: "I do not blame these men. I take all the blame on myself. Consciously I transgressed all of God's commandments. I disobeyed my parents and deceived them. I am an adulteress and a murderess. I killed my baby and wanted to kill myself. I know that I have deserved God's punishment.

"But I ask God for forgiveness. I cannot set myself free in my own strength. But I trust that Christ died for me too so that I can live for Him. I want to make a new start.

"Please help me to build my tent."

We had just finished Fatma's letter when we arrived at the airport. . . . Fatma was standing between Maurice and Timothy, turning her head in embarrassment when she saw us. . . .

"Are you shocked, Pastor?" Fatma asked.

"No, I am happy."

"Happy?"

"Yes, because there is great joy in heaven over one sinner who repents.". . .

Ingrid put her left arm around Fatma's shoulder and said: "Fatma, there are things we can never make right again. We can only place them under the cross. . . . I want to give you Jeremiah 3:14 in a very personal form, Fatma: 'Return, O faithless child, says the Lord, for I married you.'"

Without moving, Fatma sat with closed eyes. Her body was trembling slightly. Then she said:

"I'm in God's tent now, am I not?"

"Yes, this is your place. As Ingrid said, God married you."

"I shall get my things from John's house tonight," she said. . . .

"Just two more things, Fatma," I said. "First, you are free now, absolutely free. The past is effaced from God's memory. If you continue to burden yourself with your forgiven sins, you commit a new one."

"I understand."

"Second, the grace of God is like a growing light which falls into a dark room. But this is a process which goes on and on. It may well be that during the next days you will discover still more dark things in your life which you could not see today. Do not be depressed and desperate if you do. It means simply that your life is exposed to the light of God." . . .

"How do you feel, Fatma?" Ingrid asked.

She thought for a moment and then she said: "Strange, I'm alone and yet I don't feel lonely."

"That's just the point. I believe that only those should marry who are able to live alone. God wants you to prove yourself.". . .

"Poor Maurice," I muttered [later to Ingrid on the plane]. "He wanted so much to marry a virgin. And he ends up with Fatma."

Ingrid contradicted me: "But she is a virgin, Walter. She's cleansed—as the bride of Christ. 'Without spot. Without wrinkle. Without blemish.'"

Indeed, Ingrid was right.

think

- Do you agree that "only those should marry who are able to live alone"? What would you advise an emotionally mature twenty-three-year-old who wanted to get married immediately out of college? Why?
- What advice would you give to someone who wanted to remarry one year out of a previous marriage?
- Was Ingrid playing semantics with the word virgin in order to encourage Fatma in a difficult place? Or do you believe there is something deeper and authentically virginal about one made clean by Christ? Talk about this.
- Suppose you courageously reveal a "dark" part of your life to some fellow Christians. Are you more likely to receive some form of condemnation from them or some form of joy? If you've had experiences like this, talk about them.

pray

read hope!

2 Corinthians 4:8-9,16-18

> You know for yourselves that we're not much to look at. We've been surrounded and battered by troubles, but we're not demoralized; we're not sure what to do, but we know that God knows what to do; we've been spiritually terrorized, but God hasn't left our side; we've been thrown down, but we haven't broken. . . .
>
> So we're not giving up. How could we! Even though on the outside it often looks like things are falling apart on us, on the inside, where God is making new life, not a day goes by without his unfolding grace. These hard times are small potatoes compared to the coming good times, the lavish celebration prepared for us. There's far more here than meets the eye. The things we see now are here today, gone tomorrow. But the things we can't see now will last forever.

think

- Recall the circumstances surrounding the last time you felt like the first paragraph. How about the last time your marriage felt like that?
- How do you respond to times like that? Get demoralized and give up, or look ahead at the new life God is making for you? If the former, what would it take to make it the latter?
- How would you respond to one who said, "Such words are just empty cheerleading. Leaders—religious leaders, political leaders, whatever—have always distracted suffering people from their suffering by promising happiness sometime in the future."
- If you are married, has your marriage been through anything like what the apostle describes here? Have things gotten better or worse? Talk about this.

think (continued)

pray

read rebound

From *Victim of Love? How You Can Break the Cycle of Bad Relationships*, by Tom Whiteman and Randy Petersen[4]

What I needed, and what other emotionally vulnerable people need, is to allow the wounds to heal slowly—to become whole again. Just as a broken arm needs to be put in a cast, so our hearts need to be immobilized so we don't use them again before they are completely healed. And as with that broken arm, if we insist on trying to love again on a broken or wounded heart, it will only hurt all the more. If we continue to try to use it anyway, it's liable to heal crooked.

In our culture, divorce is the most common cause of what you might call catastrophic emotional vulnerability.

I knew a young man who was struggling with dissatisfaction in a dead-end job. He didn't feel significant. There was a young woman he knew who had just been through a divorce and had two young children. She desperately needed security. You could probably guess what happened. They got together for an on-again, off-again romance that held them in an addictive grip for a couple of years.

He did provide her with some security. It was great for her to know that someone loved her. And she did make him feel significant. But that's about all they did for each other. In many other ways, their affair was unhealthy. They compromised principles, ditched other friendships, and often fought with each other. . . .

It often happens as it did with [this] couple . . . : one's security is another one's significance. He felt important for being her anchor in tough times. She felt secure because he drew his significance from her. But when she needed to feel more significance, it threatened his. And when he needed security, she couldn't provide it. Their relationship was seriously tilted.

think

- Do you know anyone who resembles this scenario? If you can, talk about it.
- What is the writers' advice for healing from a terminated marriage? What might that realistically look like?
- Do you think their advice still stands even if a recently divorced person is not in a place of catastrophic emotional vulnerability?
- How do you think maritally wounded people know when they are finally healed and ready for a healthy, intimate relationship?

pray

read your time is coming

From the article "Dating after Divorce" on the website *There's Life After Divorce . . .*, by Maia Merril Berens[5]

When I left my husband, I was so wounded and confused that I didn't have much idea who I was or what marriage was really about. So the first "nice" man who paid attention to me, complimented me, asked me out—and wanted to marry me, pretty much got me. So I had a six month marriage and found out a) I didn't know much about me—but was well on my way to learning and b) I certainly didn't know what it took to make a marriage work—and was well on my way to learning. . . .

So when is it right to start dating after divorce? It's up to you. Here are some questions to ask yourself to determine whether you are really ready:

1. Can I leave my children and not feel guilty?
2. Have I begun to understand what went wrong with my marriage?
3. Am I willing to take responsibility for my part in the marriage?
4. Do I love myself?
5. Have I learned to enjoy my own company?
6. Do I have great support while I go on this new adventure with my new self?

And there are no mistakes that you can make if you remember that Life Is a School.

Isaiah 58:11-12; 62:4-5

I will always show you where to go.
I'll give you a full life in the emptiest of places—
firm muscles, strong bones.
You'll be like a well-watered garden,
a gurgling spring that never runs dry.
You'll use the old rubble of past lives to build anew,

rebuild the foundations from out of your past.
You'll be known as those who can fix anything,
restore old ruins, rebuild and renovate,
make the community livable again. . . .

No more will anyone call you Rejected,
and your country will no more be called Ruined.
You'll be called Hephzibah (My Delight),
and your land Beulah (Married),
Because God delights in you
and your land will be like a wedding celebration.
For as a young man marries his virgin bride,
so your builder marries you,
And as a bridegroom is happy in his bride,
so your God is happy with you.

think

- What is your impression of Berens' questions as a starting place for dating again?
- "I'll give you a full life in the emptiest of places"—what is your empty place now? What would a full life there look like?
- What about your life would you like to rebuild? Any ruins need restoring?
- Are you the sort that has a difficult time believing that anyone would call you "My Delight"? What would it take to convince you that God indeed loves you that tenderly?

think (continued)

pray

LIVE

what i want to discuss

What have you discovered this week that you definitely want to discuss with your small group? Write that here. Then begin your small-group discussion with these thoughts.

so what?

Use the following space to summarize what you've discovered during this chapter about starting over in a new marriage. Review your Beginning Place if you need to remember where you began. How does God's truth impact the next step in your journey?

then what?

What is one practical thing you can do to apply what you've discovered? Describe how you will put this into practice. What steps will you take? Remember to think realistically; an admirable but unreachable goal is as good as no goal. Discuss your goal with your small group to further define it.

how?

Identify how you will be held accountable to the goal you described. Who will be on your support team? What are their responsibilities? How will you measure the success of your plan? Write the details here.

hope

A new reason for living with each other

a time to review

We come to the final lesson in our *Running a Three-Legged Race Across Time* discussion guide. But this is not an ending place. With any luck (and the prayers of people who care for you), you've been discovering some truths about your life—particularly your marriage—and have seen opportunity for change. Positive change. But no matter what has brought you to this final lesson, you know that it's only a pause in your journey.

You may have uncovered behaviors or thoughts that demanded change. Perhaps you've already changed them. Will the changes stick? How will you and your spouse continue to take the momentum from this study into next week, next month, and next year? Use your time in this lesson not only to review what you discovered, but also to determine how you'll stay on track tomorrow.

You'll notice that there's a "Live" section in this lesson matched with each of the previous seven lessons. Use this to note your and your spouse's ongoing plans. Talk about your plans with small-group members. Commit your plans to prayer. And then do what you say you'll do. As you move forward with a renewed sense of purpose, you'll become more confident learning every day how better to live with your mate for better or for worse—and with the confidence will come, gradually, more success at becoming the couple you both want to become.

read expectations

Genesis 2:25

The two of them, the Man and his Wife, were naked, but they felt no shame.

think

- In what sense do you want to be naked with your spouse without feeling shame?
- What role could your faith play in achieving this desire?

pray

LIVE

How does God's truth influence the next step you'll take with your spouse in your marriage journey?

How will you take that next step?

How will you be held accountable?

read models

1 Corinthians 11:10-11

Don't, by the way, read too much into the differences here between men and women. Neither man nor woman can go it alone or claim priority. Man was created first, as a beautiful shining reflection of God—that is true. But the head on a woman's body clearly outshines in beauty the head of her "head," her husband.

think

- In what ways might you and your spouse "read too much into the differences between men and women"?
- In what ways do either (or both) of you need to reorient yourself from going it alone to practicing partnership?

pray

LIVE

How does God's truth influence the next step you'll take with your spouse in your marriage journey?

How will you take that next step?

How will you be held accountable?

read mine

1 Peter 3:7

> Be good husbands to your wives. Honor them, delight in them. As women they lack some of your advantages. But in the new life of God's grace, you're equals. Treat your wives, then, as equals so your prayers don't run aground.

think

- What advantages might the wife in your marriage lack? What advantages might the husband lack?
- What can the two of you do to equalize your marriage "in the new life of God's grace"?

pray

LIVE

How does God's truth influence the next step you'll take with your spouse in your marriage journey?

How will you take that next step?

How will you be held accountable?

read bed

1 Corinthians 7:2

Sexual drives are strong, but marriage is strong enough to contain them and provide for a balanced and fulfilling sexual life in a world of sexual disorder.

think

- In what aspect of your sex life do you and your spouse want more balance? Or from what aspect of your sex life do you want more fulfillment than you're currently receiving?
- What influence, if any, is the "world of sexual disorder" that surrounds you?

pray

LIVE

How does God's truth influence the next step you'll take with your spouse in your marriage journey?

How will you take that next step?

How will you be held accountable?

read ghosts

Ezekiel 18:19

Do you need to ask, "So why does the child not share the guilt of the parent?"

Isn't it plain? It's because the child did what is fair and right.

think

- Describe two ancestral attitudes or habits you feel yourself reliving in your own marriage.
- What has been the effect of these attitudes or habits upon your marriage?

pray

LIVE

How does God's truth influence the next step you'll take with your spouse in your marriage journey?

How will you take that next step?

How will you be held accountable?

read children

Mark 10:14

But Jesus was irate and let them know it: "Don't push these children away. Don't ever get between them and me. These children are at the very center of life in the kingdom."

think

- What are the top two ways children add tension to your marriage?
- What would it take for those child-centered marital tensions to be reduced?

pray

LIVE

How does God's truth influence the next step you'll take with your spouse in your marriage journey?

How will you take that next step?

How will you be held accountable?

read again

Isaiah 58:12; 62:5

You'll use the old rubble of past lives to build anew,
rebuild the foundations from out of your past.
You'll be known as those who can fix anything,
restore old ruins, rebuild and renovate,
make the community livable again. . . .

For as a young man marries his virgin bride,
so your builder marries you,
And as a bridegroom is happy in his bride,
so your God is happy with you.

think

- What can you see of yourself in these words of Isaiah's?
- If you've been divorced, what hope for a stable, lifelong remarriage do you have? On what is it based?

pray

LIVE

How does God's truth influence the next step you'll take with your spouse in your marriage journey?

How will you take that next step?

How will you be held accountable?

notes

lesson 1

1. Bob and Sheri Stritof, from the online "Your Guide to Marriage," http://marriage.about.com/od/marriagetoolbox/.
2. Carolyn Hax, interview by Anjula Razadan, "Advice Columnist Carolyn Hax on Intimacy Today," in "Intimacy Today," *Utne*, November/December 2004, 57.
3. John Gray, *Mars and Venus in Touch: Enhancing the Passion with Great Communication* (New York: Hallmark Books/HarperCollins, 2000), 3-4, 36.
4. Todd Temple and Jim Hancock, "Marriage" entry in *Good Advice* (Grand Rapids, Mich.: Youth Specialties/Zondervan, 1987), s.v. "marriage," 55.
5. Brennan Manning, *Abba's Child: The Cry of the Heart for Intimate Belonging* (Colorado Springs, Colo.: NavPress, 1994, 2002), 165; Interior quote from: Jüurgen Moltmann, *The Trinity and the Kingdom* (San Francisco: Harper & Row, 1981), 25, quoted in Alan Jones, *Soul Making: The Desert Way of Spirituality* (San Francisco: Harper & Row).
6. Carol Kent, *Secret Longings of the Heart* (Colorado Springs, Colo.: NavPress, 2003), 116-117.

lesson 2

1. Nina Utne, "Dancing with Monogamy," *Utne,* November/December 2004, 6.
2. Jeannette Cooperman, "Many Models of Marriage Can and Do Exist," *National Catholic Reporter*, January 23, 2004, http://www.highbeam .com/library/docfree.asp?DOCID=1G1:112861783&num=5&ctrlInfo=Round18 %3AMode18c%3ASR%3AResult&ao=&FreePremium=BOTH.
3. from www.highbeam.com. Glenn T. Stanton, *Why Marriage Matters: Reasons to Believe in Marriage in a Postmodern Society* (Colorado Springs, Colo.: Piñon Press, 1997), 166, 12.

lesson 3

1. Madeleine L'Engle, *Two-Part Invention: The Story of a Marriage* (San Francisco: Harper & Row, 1988).
2. Kahlil Gibran, *The Prophet*, "On Marriage" (New York: Knopf, 1923), 15-16.
3. Anita Diamant, *The Red Tent* (New York: Picador, 1997), 62, 158, 175.
4. Carol Kent, *Secret Longings of the Heart* (Colorado Springs, Colo.: NavPress, 2003), 149-150.

lesson 4

1. Jeremiah Creedon, "Everything You Always Wanted to Know ..., " *Utne*, September/October, 2003, 72.
2. Vanes Naldi and Mike Lorefice, review of *Three Colors: Red*, directed by Krzysztof Kiewlowski, July 25, 2005, http://www.metalasylum.com/raging-bull/movies/threecolorsred.html www.metalasylum.com.
3. Kevin Leman, *Becoming a Couple of Promise* (Colorado Springs, Colo.: NavPress, 1999), 40-41.
4. Esther Perel, "In Search of Erotic Intelligence: Reconciling Sensuality and Domesticity," *Psychotherapy Networker*, May/June 2003, Vol. 27, Issue 3, http://pqasb.pqarchiver.com/psychotherapynetworker/671612621.html?did=671612621&FMT=ABS&FMTS=FT&date=May%2FJun+2003&author=Esther+Perel&pub=Psychotherapy+Networker&desc=Erotic+Intelligence.
5. David Bowie to Greg Kot, Knight Ridder News Service, in *The Oregonian*, August 13, 2002.

lesson 5

1. Laura Tohe, "A Woman's Place," *ASU Research*, Summer 2003, http://researchmag.asu.edu/articles/Tohe.html.
2. Kevin Leman, *Becoming a Couple of Promise* (Colorado Springs, Colo.: NavPress, 1999), 47, 29.
3. Maggie Scarf, *Intimate Partners: Patterns in Love and Marriage* (New York: Ballantine, 1987), 179-181.
4. Frederick Buechner, *The Sacred Journey: A Memoir of Early Days* (San Francisco: Harper & Row, 1982), 83-85.

lesson 6

1. Madeleine L'Engle, *Two-Part Invention: The Story of a Marriage* (San Francisco: Harper & Row, 1988), 181.
2. Mary Pipher, *The Shelter of Each Other* (New York: Grosset/Putnam, 1996), 191.
3. Lois Romano, "Branson, Mo., Looks Beyond RVs and Buffets: Prosperous Conservative Movement Has Blue-Collar Retreat Aiming to Go Upscale," *Washington Post*, August 8, 2005, A3, http://www.washingtonpost.com/wp-dyn/content/article/2005/08/07/AR2005080700873.html.

4. Jim Hancock, *Raising Adults: Getting Kids Ready for the Real World* (Colorado Springs, Colo.: Piñon Press, 1999), 126.

lesson 7

1. Robert Farrar Capon, *The Romance of the Word: One Man's Love Affair with Theology* (Grand Rapids, Mich.: Eerdmans, 1995), 6.
2. Rose Sweet, *How to Be First in a Second Marriage* (Joplin, Mo.: College Press Publishing Co., 1999), n.p.
3. Walter Trobisch, *I Married You* (InterVarsity, 1971), 153-157, 159.
4. Tom Whiteman and Randy Petersen, *Victim of Love? How You Can Break the Cycle of Bad Relationships* (Colorado Springs, Colo.: Piñon Press, 1998), 101-102.
5. Maia Merril Berens, "Dating after Divorce," *There's Life After Divorce* website www.theres-life-after-divorce.com.

First comes love, then comes marriage, then comes...hard work?

In one word, describe your marriage. If you answered anything other than "perfect," you need the honest truth from this new Bible discussion guide on staying married in a culture hostile to marriage.

The eight lessons of *Running a Three-Legged Race Across Time* feature literary and cultural insights, conversation starters, and key passages from the best-selling *Message* Bible. Each chapter is an open, free-flowing discussion about a tricky issue many married couples encounter (and ignore at their own peril).

Running a Three-Legged Race Across Time avoids stale, glib answers and instead points you toward honest questions that every couple should be asking themselves. Read it together, read it on your own, but take a little time to think about your marriage—and how to stay married till death do you part.

Also available from the REAL LIFE STUFF FOR COUPLES series:

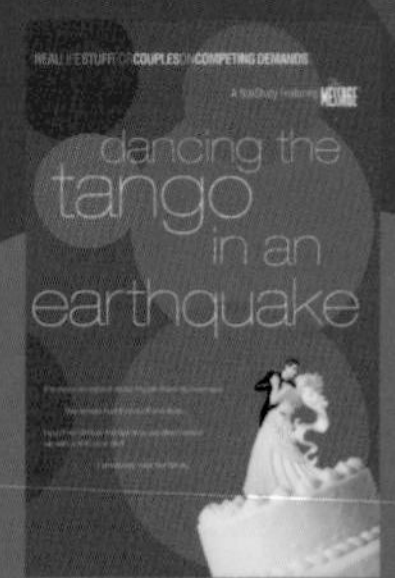

On Competing Demands

ISBN 1-60006-018-8

NAVPRESS®
BRINGING TRUTH TO LIFE
www.navpress.com